NEGOTIATING
POWER

A 360° Strategy For
Leadership, Labor & Legacy

by L. R. DeFell, Esq., MPA

NEGOTIATING POWER: A 360° Strategy for Leadership, Labor & Legacy by L. R. DeFell, Esq., MPA

ISBN: 978-8-9939105-0-5

Published by LRD360° Press
Publisher@lrd360.com
Illinois, United States

"*The greatest test of leadership is not how loud you speak for others, but how well you listen to them.*"

~ *César Chávez*

Dedication

For those who negotiate not for power, but for people. For the ones who sit in the silence between sentences. You know the pressure, the politics, and the purpose behind every pause. This is for you, the unseen leaders who turn conflict into progress and pressure into trust.

Acknowledgments

To the mentors, peers, and colleagues who taught me that progress is built one honest conversation at a time. To my family, whose steadiness made every late-night and overnight bargaining session possible. And to every leader willing to listen longer than they speak — this book is your echo.

About the Author

L. R. DeFell, Esq., MPA, is a seasoned strategist, negotiator, and advocate whose career bridges public-sector management and union-side labor relations, executive contracts, and leadership cultures in organizations where power, people, and purpose must coexist. She was born and raised in Chicago, where she writes, mentors emerging leaders, and continues to champion the art of principled negotiation.

Contents

PREFACE
The Courage to Lead

Leadership is not tested in calm moments; it's revealed in the turbulence between them. True leadership emerges when conditions shift: when the ground falters and every voice in the room demands attention.

No two challenges are the same, but one truth holds: Progress never happens by autopilot.

Leadership is not about dominance or bravado. It's balancing **Loyalty**, **Respect**, and **Dignity** in every decision when pressure peaks and the stakes escalate.

I've spent decades navigating rooms where every word carried the weight of livelihoods — bargaining tables that resembled battlefields, boardrooms pulsating with politics, and moments when silence itself became a measure of resolve.

The lessons gathered here aren't theories; they're lived experiences. Every contract signed, every crisis resolved, and every turning point endured has shaped a simple truth: Leadership is not about surviving the moment — it's about defining it.

This book, *Negotiating Power: A 360° Strategy for Leadership, Labor, and Legacy*, was born from those experiences. It's not an academic treatise or a corporate manual. It's a lived reflection on what it means to lead people — not just policies — through pressure, conflict, and change.

LRD360° is more than a framework; it's a perspective. It's how we move — with Loyalty, Respect, and Dignity — through negotiations, leadership, and life. These aren't slogans. They're anchors. They center you when everything else seems unstable.

You'll see the lessons of labor applied well beyond the bargaining table — in crisis management, leadership transitions, organizational transformation, and in how cultures are built and trust restored. You'll also find parallels between the public sector and professional sports, health care, and finance, as well as legacy challenges and new frontiers where leadership, labor, and legacy intersect.

Whether you're negotiating a collective bargaining agreement or an executive sports contract, or rebuilding a fractured workplace culture, the principles remain the same. Know your value. Honor the process. Protect the people.

This isn't a book about avoiding storms. It's about standing firm within them — reading the shifts, trusting your

preparation, and leading with courage even as the path ahead unfolds.

LRD360° Insight: True leadership isn't about predicting the future; it's about preparing people to meet it.

CHAPTER 1

The Art of Alignment

Power, Permission, and the Politics of Public-Sector Negotiation

Where Power First Meets Purpose

So here we are: two opposing sides facing each other across a narrow table but separated by a world of purpose.

One side holds ten uniformed officers in tactical vests, men trained to read threat and control chaos. Every day, they move through danger most people only read about.

Their posture is unflinching, their eyes fixed. Behind them stand thirty-five more, elected stewards, quiet but imposing, carrying the weight of the membership that sent them here.

The air is dense with tension, not anger; the kind of pressure that makes the room feel smaller than it is. It's the silence of calculation, of waiting. You can almost hear the shift of fabric, the controlled breath behind every stare. It feels like standing between hungry men and their next meal. It's not personal; it's instinct.

Our side looks smaller. Seven suits.

I serve as Chief Strategist and Spokesperson, surrounded by professionals who know their craft: my outside counsel, a legal gladiator with precision that could slice through ambiguity; two subject-matter experts who know the operations down to the wire; and staff who capture every word and nuance. We don't carry armor, but we don't need to. Preparation is our defense; discipline, our weapon.

It's impossible to tell at first who leads the other side. There are no introductions, no nameplates. Leadership reveals itself through rhythm: whom others watch before they speak, whose nod ends a sidebar. Experience teaches you to recognize power long before it announces itself.

The first moments are choreography. Who sits first. Who breaks eye contact. Who speaks without being asked. In collective bargaining, you learn early that every gesture means something.

So, I step forward, deliberate and steady, and extend my hand, not to the lawyer but to the leader. I don't need confirmation to know who that is. The room exhales, barely. Respect offered. Respect returned.

How Power Behaves Under Pressure

What happens next isn't just a negotiation; it's a lesson in how power behaves when purpose collides with pressure.

To understand these dynamics, let's consider how power operates in such moments.

Power doesn't always roar across the table; sometimes it hums quietly in the pauses between sentences. In collective bargaining, power is rarely about volume. It's about preparation, posture, and perception.

Every side walks in with a different kind of power.

The union's power lives in numbers, in solidarity, in the threat of disruption, in the moral high ground of protecting the worker. Management's power lives in responsibility: to taxpayers, to budgets, to sustaining the enterprise beyond one contract cycle.

Power without permission becomes arrogance. Permission without boundaries becomes chaos. Leadership lives in the space between the two.

That's the quiet labor of the Chief Spokesperson: understanding that the process isn't just about wages and benefits; it's about trust. You lead by reading tone as carefully as you read numbers.

LRD360° Insight: Data wins arguments, but tone wins outcomes.

The Anatomy of Power: How Preparation, Position, and Performance Shape Leadership

When you strip away titles and talking points, bargaining is about legitimacy. Who has earned the right to speak and be believed.

In my experience, legitimacy comes from three things:

1. Preparation: knowing every clause, every budget line, every historical context before you open your mouth.

2. Position: understanding the authority you represent and its limits.

3. Performance: proving, through consistency and clarity, that you can be trusted with solutions that affect thousands.

These three form the spine of leadership. Miss one, and the body collapses.

So, when the union president begins to outline their opening proposal, citing morale, safety, parity, I listen for what's beneath the words. Not the demands themselves, but the values driving them. Sometimes, it's fairness. Sometimes, respect. Sometimes, just acknowledgment that their work matters.

Understanding why they fight makes you more effective in choosing what to fight for.

But even the best preparation and position mean little without something deeper: permission. Not the kind granted by authority, but the kind earned quietly through trust.

In leadership, power may open the door, but permission is what allows you to stay in the room.

Permission: The Quiet Currency of Leadership

Permission is a misunderstood form of power. In the public sector, permission doesn't come from a CEO or a shareholder. It comes from the public itself, from taxpayers who expect balance: fair treatment of workers and responsible stewardship of funds.

That means every concession exacts a double cost: one on paper and one in optics.

LRD360° Insight: In government bargaining, every dollar has two owners: the worker and the taxpayer.

To navigate that, you must earn permission twice: once from leadership and once from public trust. That's why I spend as much time communicating about why decisions were made as well as what decisions were made. Transparency is not a courtesy — it's a currency.

And perception, once granted, quickly becomes politics. Because the moment permission becomes visible, it invites interpretation and interpretation becomes the story.

The Politics of Perception: Managing the Story Before It Manages You

Politics is the shadow that follows every negotiation. Not partisan politics, though party lines eventually shape outcomes, but the politics of perception.

In the public sector, every agreement is judged long before it is understood. Headlines and hashtags shape opinions faster than facts:

- "Management caves to union demands."

- "Union wins big at taxpayer expense."

- "Union gets sweetheart deal."

Each media headline tells part of the story. Partial stories erode trust.

That's why managing perception is as critical as managing resources. You must define the narrative before others do, articulating intent and impact with precision and restraint.

LRD360° Insight: If you don't tell your story, someone else will, and they'll tell it wrong.

We learned that lesson firsthand. In one of the most challenging bargaining cycles of my career, we negotiated a concessionary contract: an agreement in which one side gives up something it previously won and values, usually for the benefit of the organization or the greater good. The kind of agreement every leader on both sides dreads.

The organization was hemorrhaging financially, and survival required asking employees to give something back: a step increase, a raise, or contractual language with economic implications. These are extraordinarily difficult conversations that only succeed through deep trust, transparency, and strategic empathy.

We achieved the impossible; a deal built on mutual respect and shared sacrifice. Yet in focusing so intently on building trust, we underestimated the power of optics.

Employees gave a concession, earned through difficult negotiation and intended to benefit the organization. Yet the media spun it as a "union sweetheart deal." The outrage was swift, and the truth was lost in translation.

Politics will always test principle. Leadership begins with how you respond to that test.

That moment cemented a lasting leadership principle: Perception is part of the work, not a distraction from it. Managing it with foresight and discipline is as vital as the negotiation itself.

Where Leadership Lives: Acting When No One Else Will

By the end of that first day, nothing is signed. The officers pack their binders; the suits gather their notes. The silence that once pressed in now shifts to fatigue. But the real work has only begun.

The session has ended, but leadership has begun.

True leadership isn't measured by who spoke the longest or pressed the hardest. It's revealed in what remains when the talking stops: trust, credibility, and the courage to act when something is wrong.

During one session, a steward raised a critical issue: Management had begun canceling overtime for nurses who had called off sick the prior week, including employees with approved Family and Medical Leave.

This was no minor oversight; it touched on fairness, morale, and compliance. We acted immediately. Within an hour, we corrected the practice, retrained the responsible manager, and communicated transparently with affected staff.

By addressing it in real time, we reinforced the principles of fairness, accountability, and trust.

LRD360° Insight: Integrity is not situational; it's a discipline.

That moment reaffirmed what leadership demands: the courage to act decisively and quietly when principle is at stake.

The art of leadership lies not in domination. It is disciplined execution, respecting the other side's dignity even when you disagree, in holding your own team accountable when the facts don't favor you, and in walking away from the table with relationships intact, because tomorrow, you may need them again.

LRD360° Insight: Every agreement is temporary. Every relationship is permanent.

The Human Psychology of Negotiation: What Numbers Can't See

No matter how technical the data or complex the term, bargaining always comes down to one element: people.

People with fears, families, ambitions, and the quiet needs to be respected.

I've seen perfectly balanced offers rejected for reasons that had nothing to do with numbers. Sometimes it's pride. Sometimes it's a scar from a past negotiation. Sometimes it's the simple fact that the other side felt unheard.

Consider one of the union's chief stewards. She had survived an unauthorized reorganization that resulted in layoffs. Though the union ultimately won arbitration and employees were reinstated, it took a year — a year separated from coworkers, paychecks, and identity.

That year left a scar.

When she returned to the table as chief steward, the air was charged. Every proposal, no matter how fair or logical, was filtered through the memory of that loss.

One misjudged remark could ignite her anger and ripple through the rest of the stewards.

You could feel it in the room: tension like a pin balanced on a grenade, one wrong move away from detonation.

It was a reminder that negotiations aren't won on paper; they're won in the hearts and minds of the people at the table.

LRD360° Insight: You're never just negotiating a contract. You're negotiating trust.

Reading the Room: The Silent Data of Human Behavior

You can't teach instinct, but you can train awareness.

When you sit at the table long enough, you start to recognize patterns: how frustration hides behind sarcasm, how confidence slips into silence.

Watch the eyes. The ones who speak least often hold the most power.

Watch the hands. When they stop writing notes, they've stopped listening.

These are micro-moments of truth: small tells that reveal where resistance is building and where empathy is needed.

In labor relations, emotional literacy isn't a soft skill; it's a survival skill.

Every time I enter a bargaining room, I remind myself of two truths:

1. No one wants to lose.
2. No one wants to be embarrassed.

Respect those, and you can navigate almost anything.

LRD360° Insight: Emotional literacy is the strategist's most undervalued advantage.

Managing Ego Without Losing Ground

Ego isn't the enemy. Unmanaged ego is.

Every leader brings it. It's part of what put them in the chair. The danger begins when ego becomes identity.

Logic fades. Proposals are heard as insults. Corrections feel like attacks. The room stops negotiating and starts defending.

In one session, a manager insisted that the department had never denied a vacation request due to staffing. A steward quietly presented evidence of the opposite: A denial notice time-stamped and verified.

Rather than acknowledge the mistake, the manager doubled down with excuses. His credibility shrank in real time.

Moments like that demand decisive leadership. I called a caucus, realigned the team, and refocused the conversation on facts, not pride.

A Chief Strategist's job is to keep the table tethered to purpose, not personality. That means defusing tension, not matching it; redirecting dialogue, not retaliating.

When ego is managed and purpose stays centered, credibility strengthens, and progress returns.

LRD360° Insight: When ego drives the table, the deal crashes.

The Psychology of Momentum: Turning Movement into Meaning

Negotiation is rhythm. You build it, you lose it, you recover it.

Momentum is what transforms a conversation into a conclusion.

Every proposal and counterproposal is a chance to move the story forward.

If one side feels stalled, resentment grows. If both feel progress, trust deepens.

That's why I design bargaining sessions around psychological milestones, not just financial ones. Small early agreements build confidence.

They create forward motion, which is proof that progress is possible.

In one session, we resolved a simple but long-standing issue: clarifying overtime approval procedures. It required no new funding but eliminated daily frustration for hundreds of employees. The stewards saw that their concerns were heard. Management saw that the process worked.

That single success changed the tone of the room. It gave everyone something tangible to point to, momentum they could feel.

Clarifying shared values before diving into dollars reminded everyone why they were there.

Momentum isn't about speed; it's about direction. Even slow movement beats standing still.

When nurtured intentionally, momentum transforms a tense, guarded table into a space where trust grows, collaboration emerges, and the final agreement feels earned by everyone involved.

LRD360° Insight: Progress doesn't require speed. It requires shared direction.

The Human Element: Where Strategy Meets Empathy

What makes the LRD360° approach different isn't just the analysis. It's the anthropology.

I study behavior as closely as I study budgets.

Fear of loss often outweighs hope of gain. A small gesture of respect can outweigh a five-figure proposal. And one careless word can unravel a year's worth of trust.

Leadership is measured not in numbers, but in human impact.

During one negotiation, a manager in caucus dismissed administrative assistants as "nothing but glorified secretaries."

The timing couldn't have been worse. The stewards, who had just walked back into the room, heard every word.

Disbelief. Deflation. Anger.

One careless comment threatened to undo hours of progress.

The lesson was immediate: Words carry weight equal to dollars, and respect is a nonnegotiable clause in every agreement.

People remember how you made them feel long after they forget the final number. That memory becomes the starting point for the next round.

That's why, before every session, I ask myself two questions:

1. What outcome do I want?
2. What feeling do I want to leave in the room?

When those two answers align, you're leading, not just negotiating.

LRD360° Insight: Strategy wins the deal; empathy sustains it.

The Leader at the Table

When the last word fades and both teams pack away their notes, the energy shifts.

The hum of debate becomes stillness. That silence is the true measure of leadership.

In every negotiation, there comes a point when authority is no longer enough.

What defines a leader then isn't power. It's composure: The ability to stay centered when the room sways toward volatility.

Anyone can dominate a table; few can steady one.

The LRD360° framework calls this situational anchoring: The discipline to remain grounded while everything else moves.

It's not emotional detachment; it's emotional discipline.

You listen. You assess. You influence. But you do not absorb the chaos.

That's the difference between a technician and a strategist.

LRD360° Insight: You cannot lead a table you're emotionally seated at.

A Chief Strategist's greatest test is invisible: holding steady while everyone else reaches for the wheel.

It means knowing when to pivot from defense to dialogue, when to let silence speak for you, and when to remind both sides that the table exists not for victory, but for balance.

Preparation, logic, and data build the scaffolding of the deal. But tone, perception, and timing determine whether that scaffolding holds.

You can have the strongest numbers in the room and still lose the moment if you fail to read its pulse.

Leadership at the table is both science and intuition. Choreography between empathy and authority.

By the time I leave that first day's session, I'm already mapping the second: posture, sequence, and tone, noting where trust grew and where tension spiked.

Those notes become tomorrow's strategy.

A principal, the person who hired me, once asked my strategy for bargaining.

I smiled and said, "I won't know until I get to the table."

Because strategy isn't written in ink. It's felt in the room; in pauses, glances, and shifts in tone.

True leadership is iterative.

Each meeting is a diagnostic: a reflection of whether you led with intellect or instinct, control or collaboration.

The table is a mirror. It reflects back your discipline, your patience, and your respect for process.

LRD360° Insight: Every table teaches the cost of unguarded emotion and the value of measured silence.

When you understand that, you stop negotiating for closure and start negotiating for continuity.

Because every agreement is only as sustainable as the trust it preserves.

That is the true art of the deal: creating peace that outlasts the paper it's written on.

Closing Reflection

Every negotiation begins as a test of knowledge, but ends as a measure of presence.

Power isn't declared by how loudly you argue but by how quietly you hold the room. When preparation and principle align, leadership becomes less about victory and more about stewardship.

LRD360° Insight: Power that isn't grounded in purpose eventually turns on itself.

From the Table to the People

Every negotiation ends the same way it begins: with people.

The contracts, numbers, and talking points are only surface evidence of something older and deeper: the human instinct to seek fairness when structure fails to deliver it.

The bargaining table may define the tactics, but the why behind every bargaining session lives outside the room: in break rooms, patrol cars, classrooms, and hospital corridors where policy meets reality.

That's where unions are born. Not from anger, but from absence: absence of trust, absence of voice, absence of dignity.

The next chapter begins there, in the moment before the table even exists, when workers decide that the only way to be heard is to stand together.

Because before you can understand negotiation, you have to understand why people organize in the first place.

LRD360° Insight: Negotiation is the art of response; unionization is the language of need.

CHAPTER 2

Why People Unionize
The Human Equation in Practice

Where Needs Become Narratives and Narratives Become Movements

Before a union ever forms, a whisper always comes first.

It begins as quiet discontent: a hallway sigh, a closed-door conversation, an unanswered email that meant more than the sender intended.

That's how every movement starts: not with rebellion, but with recognition that someone stopped listening.

If Chapter 1 was about what happens once the table is set, this chapter is about what forces people to build a new one.

The Union Recognition Petition Email Arrives

The ping of an inbox rarely carries the weight of history, but this one did.

Subject: Notice of Union Representation Petition: Human Resources Division.

For a moment, the room froze. Coffee cups hovered mid-air. Screens blinked in quiet disbelief.

HR, the department, built to recruit others to the organization, manage fairness, and resolve disputes, had now filed its own petition to be represented by a union.

The strategist read the line twice, not because the words were unclear, but because they struck something deeper: If even HR had lost faith in management, what was left to steward?

Outside the window, late-afternoon light hit the downtown towers at an angle that made everything look suspended: contracts, confidence, even calm.

The legal team, already exhausted from months of bargaining across multiple agencies, gathered instinctively.

No one spoke at first.

Then someone whispered what everyone was thinking:

"If they've unionized HR, the message isn't about money."

The Leadership Reckoning

The strategist leaned back, recalling how each petition over the years had been a fire signal.

The doctors: brilliant, burned-out, and tired of being told how to heal.

The pharmacists: disciplined professionals who'd lost autonomy to algorithms and cost-cutting protocols.

The nurses: stretched between compassion and compliance, whose empathy had finally turned to exhaustion.

And now, the Human Resources staff, the supposed guardians of dignity, had crossed the same line.

What began as scattered sparks of dissatisfaction had become an undeniable pattern: When people no longer feel heard, they organize to be seen.

Lawyers were dispatched like courtiers to brief executives, not on the law, but on the optics.

Press statements were drafted, meetings scheduled, whispers contained.

But inside the strategist's mind, a quieter truth formed: This wasn't about contracts or classifications. It was about trust, the currency every institution spends fastest and replenishes slowest.

Flashbacks replayed like quick cuts from a documentary:

The physician who once said, "We were trained to save lives, not fight budgets."

The pharmacist who stayed after her shift to explain that all she wanted was "a voice in scheduling."

The nurse who held a patient's hand for hours while a grievance hearing waited downstairs.

And somewhere in that chain of moments, the strategist realized the warning signs had been there all along, not in data, but in tone.

The HR petition, though, felt like a mirror turned inward.

If the custodians of culture needed representation, leadership had missed the message completely.

It wasn't betrayal; it was feedback, only louder, costlier, and now public.

The Leadership Response

Leadership didn't need another meeting; it needed a reckoning.

The CEO called within minutes. "We can't fix this with memos," he said. And he was right. This wasn't an employee issue; it was a credibility issue.

As the dust settled, the decision was made to centralize labor oversight, not as a power grab, but as protection: to unify policy, restore trust, and stop leaders from contradicting each other across departments.

Real alignment demanded action, not announcement.

Quietly, we replaced local managers who had allowed small indignities to grow into collective anger. The move wasn't punishment; it was triage, to restore credibility where neglect had taken root.

We didn't centralize labor overnight, but by the next budget cycle, the framework was taking shape.

Systems fail at their weakest point, and in this case, it was the failure to listen.

That night, long after the office emptied, the strategist stayed behind.

The city outside still pulsed. Ambulances somewhere. Distant sirens from the same hospitals where so many had organized.

The document sat open: "Post-Petition Strategy," a title that felt heavier than the words beneath it.

The strategist began typing, not legal arguments, but questions:

- Where did the breakdown start?

- When did feedback become rebellion?

- Who stopped listening first?

The cursor blinked again, waiting.

In the rhythm of that silence, an insight formed:

"Union petitions are rarely the beginning of unrest; they're the evidence that leadership missed the preamble."

And so, before the next bargaining session, before the next petition or press call, one truth settled in like evening light across the desk: When people no longer feel seen, they create a new table, their own forum for decisions, influence, and dignity.

Tomorrow would bring statements, strategy decks, and perhaps panic.

But tonight brought clarity, the kind that changes how you lead.

That petition was never just about one workplace or one vote.

It was evidence of what happens when everyday concerns go unanswered for too long.

LRD360° Insight: When fairness feels unattainable inside the system, people look outside it for power.

Bread and Butter / Respect and Dignity: Two Sides of the Same Coin

Every organizing story has its spark, but the real ignition is almost always the same: bread and butter, or respect and dignity.

Two sides of the same coin: one feeds the body; the other feeds the soul.

That's where every union story truly begins.

It's rarely anger that starts a union. It's the quiet math of comparison.

Numbers whispered across cubicles.

Lunch-table confessions that begin with "Do you know what they're paying at …?"

What starts as curiosity turns into clarity. And clarity, once shared, becomes movement.

Bread and Butter: The Technology Team

The tech team were good people: smart, loyal, the ones who could make the system hum again when everyone else was panicking.

They adored their supervisor, enjoyed hybrid schedules, and worked on cutting-edge systems.

They laughed together in stand-ups and had built a culture of camaraderie that most leaders would envy.

Birthdays were remembered. Wins were celebrated.

The supervisors treated their staff with a level of respect rarely seen in technical departments.

The only problem was the pay.

Over the years, market rates climbed while the organization's salary tables stood still.

HR promised a compensation study "next quarter."

Finance said the budget was tight.

The employees believed them, at first.

But inflation crept in.

Rents rose.

Friends in the private sector started landing jobs with twenty-percent signing bonuses and fully remote schedules.

It wasn't resentment that broke the calm; it was reality.

One afternoon, a systems analyst pulled up Glassdoor during lunch.

The screen showed a number — thirty thousand dollars higher than their own salary for the same job title two blocks away.

Someone laughed.

Then someone else didn't.

By the end of the week, the chatter had spread.

"We love this place, but love doesn't pay the mortgage."

When leadership finally launched the salary survey, the results confirmed what the staff already knew: They were behind. Woefully behind.

That's when the first organizing call went out.

Within months, signatures followed.

The irony?

The tech staff didn't want to leave. They wanted to stay.

The petition wasn't rebellion; it was preservation.

They were saying, "We want to keep working here, but we also want to live."

LRD360° Insight: When wages stall, loyalty becomes a luxury item.

The Generational Reality Check

Gen Z doesn't wait for promises to mature.

They were raised in a world where pay transparency is public and mobility is easy.

To them, collective action isn't radical; it's rational.

They'll organize before they beg, and they'll walk before they warn.

In the end, the organization gained something unexpected.

Once represented, the tech team stayed.

Their petition was the best possible outcome because it forced the employer to reconcile compensation with reality.

Bargaining was less costly than turnover.

The lesson was clear: When employees choose to organize instead of quit, you still have a chance to lead.

That's the bread-and-butter side: When compensation fails to match contribution, people stop feeling valued and start feeling used.

Culture can't compensate for inequity; it only delays its exposure.

LRD360° Insight: Market data is your early-warning system. Ignore it, and you'll negotiate with it later at a premium.

Respect and Dignity: The White-Collar Disconnect

If bread and butter keep the body alive, respect and dignity keep the spirit whole.

These are trickier currencies; they don't appear on pay stubs or budget spreadsheets, yet they decide whether people give you their best or just their compliance.

Many assume that health care professionals unionize only when pushed to extremes, such as during pandemics, burnout waves, or moral-injury moments.

But the physicians I worked with formed their union long before COVID ever became a word on the evening news.

These were doctors who had weathered public-health crises from HIV to Ebola.

They weren't demanding more money; they were demanding a voice.

They'd spent years practicing through emergencies, following ever-changing protocols written without their input.

Division chiefs and veteran physicians, people who once scoffed at the idea of unionizing, eventually signed cards not for greed, but for governance.

They wanted respect and dignity baked into decision-making, not sprinkled on afterward.

The lesson: Bread and butter keep you fed; respect and dignity keep you whole.

And yet, this wasn't confined to medicine.

Attorneys were being dispatched like couriers, sprinting between courthouses across the county, covering multiple dockets a day as if their legal expertise were a delivery route.

Pharmacists were mandated to work every weekend, every holiday, missing family moments because "that's how we've always done it."

Nurses rotated through critical patients back-to-back without relief.

Across professions, exhaustion had become currency.

When someone finally said, "Suck it up, that's why you make the big bucks," something in the room shifted. What had been quiet frustration started hardening into collective will.

LRD360° Insight: When people feel unseen or unheard, they don't walk out; they organize.

The Tipping Point of Dignity

These employees didn't organize out of entitlement.

They did it because the balance between bread and butter, and respect and dignity, had tipped too far for too long.

If "bread and butter" fuels organizing in technical and trade roles, "respect and dignity" ignites it in professional ranks.

It's less about the paycheck and more about the posture across the table.

Take the nurse leader who had weathered three reorganizations in five years.

Each time, new executives arrived with new ideas, holding "listening sessions" that weren't really listening.

Her expertise was politely acknowledged, then quietly overwritten.

Her title changed twice; her input changed nothing.

Or the policy analyst who built an award-winning program, only to see the credit redirected in a press release to someone two levels above.

"It's fine," she said at first.

But over time, fine turned into fatigue.

White-collar professionals rarely organize over dollars; they organize over dignity.

It happens when the hallway thank-yous stop, when feedback becomes one-directional, when the word team starts to sound like a slogan instead of a promise.

A union card, in that moment, is less about wages and more about worth.

It's a declaration:

"If you won't acknowledge my contribution, I'll create a structure that does."

LRD360° Insight: People don't organize for power; they organize for proof that their work matters.

Reading the Room: Rebalancing the Equation

When people organize, leaders often ask, "Why now?"

The truth is, the warning signs were always there — whispered in engagement surveys, buried in exit interviews, hinted at in the tone of an email that said, "per my last message."

The real question isn't why now, but why didn't we notice sooner?

Unions don't appear overnight; they grow in the soil of silence.

Every time leadership dismisses a concern as trivial, every time a manager enforces a rule unevenly, another root takes hold.

By the time petitions arrive, the forest has already grown; you just failed to see the canopy forming above you.

LRD360° Insight: You can't manage what you refuse to measure; and morale is measurable if you're listening.

In one large medical system I advised, leadership launched an ambitious innovation initiative.

They poured millions into new equipment, upgraded electronic records, redesigned waiting rooms, and rolled out a flashy employee-wellness app.

Yet beneath all the progress metrics, employees felt forgotten.

The nurses still couldn't get vacation approvals processed on time.

Techs still had no voice in scheduling changes.

So, when the union came knocking, they opened the door, politely at first, then proudly.

Not because they opposed progress, but because they wanted to be part of defining it.

There are three words that will create a positive or negative environment: Consistency, Stability, and Equity. The triad every leader must uphold.

- Consistency keeps decisions fair.
- Stability builds confidence.
- Equity preserves dignity.

Break any one of the three pillars and unrest begins.

A supervisor who bends a rule for one favorite employee but disciplines another for the same act has just lit a match.

An HR team that takes three months to process one pay raise and three days for another has poured gasoline on it.

The goal isn't perfection; it's pattern.

Employees can forgive mistakes. What they won't forgive is favoritism.

LRD360° Insight: Leadership equity isn't about treating everyone the same; it's about explaining why differences exist.

The Quiet Warnings Leaders Can't Ignore

Unions are signals, not enemies. They appear when issues have been ignored too long.

By the time a petition arrives, the data was already there but ignored:

- Rising FMLA requests signaling burnout.
- Higher use of sick time and personal days.

- Exit interviews citing "lack of growth" or "culture mismatch."
- Grievance upticks

Every one of these is an early alarm.

But management, chasing budgets and deadlines, often treats them as operational noise.

LRD360° Insight: Unionization isn't rebellion; it's feedback delivered at scale.

Leaders who listen early rarely face petitions.

They hold skip-level meetings: conversations where leaders meet directly with employees two or more levels below them, bypassing their immediate managers to hear concerns firsthand.

They publish the compensation study before employees ask.

They make sure every department has a path for input that isn't filtered through fear.

Listening doesn't weaken management; it stabilizes it.

And when the conversation happens before the petition, the outcome is collaboration, not confrontation.

So, They've Unionized: Now What?

In labor relations, the difference between chaos and collaboration often comes down to one word: approach.

Leaders who view the union as an obstacle get resistance.

Leaders who view it as a feedback system get results.

This is where leadership is tested. Where tension must turn into trust, and opposition must evolve into partnership.

From Defensiveness to Partnership

The moment employees organize, leadership faces a choice: Defend the status quo or redefine it.

The first reaction is almost always emotional.

I've seen CEOs clench their fists, department heads pace, HR teams whisper "How could they?" as if unionization were betrayal.

But the truth is, it's feedback, in its loudest form.

And feedback, no matter how uncomfortable, is still a gift.

Many executives respond to early union signs by circling the wagons: calling legal, tightening policies, rehearsing talking points.

But defensiveness only confirms the perception that leadership can't be trusted.

The leaders who last, the ones whose organizations weather transitions gracefully, use unions to their advantage.

They recognize that organized labor can be a lens, not a menace.

Your favorite actor, pilot, TV anchor, and nurse all belong to unions.

They are part of the American fabric.

Consider a large nonprofit health care system employing more than 230,000 people nationwide, and nearly 180,000 are unionized. The ratio mirrors that of Cook County, Illinois, one of the nation's largest public-sector employers, where approximately eighty percent of the workforce is covered under collective bargaining agreements.

If you can't lead in a unionized environment, you can't lead where America works.

The leaders who recognize that move from fear to strategy.

They stop seeing us versus them and start asking, "What are they trying to tell us that we failed to hear?"

LRD360° Insight: Unionization is not mutiny; it's communication that went unanswered too long.

Reframing the Narrative

When I counsel executives after a successful union election, my first directive is simple: Stop calling it a loss.

If you frame the outcome as defeat, you'll lead defensively.

If you frame it as transition, you'll lead deliberately.

One public-sector director I coached used to begin every meeting with the phrase, "Now that they've gone union …"

I stopped him mid-sentence.

"Try this," I said. "Now that we're a represented organization."

That one change shifted everything.

Language matters.

It determines posture.

Posture determines trust.

When leadership replaces separation with shared identity, employees start to test that possibility, to see whether management actually means it.

LRD360° Insight: Respect begins with the words you choose when no one is grading your tone.

Data + Dialogue: The Dual Engines of Trust

After union formation, both sides are flooded with assumptions.

Management fears the budget will explode.

Employees fear management will retaliate.

Facts dissolve both.

One of my favorite strategies is the Transparency Table, a standing monthly meeting where labor and management share basic operational data: overtime usage, vacancy rates, turnover trends, and safety incidents with their new union partners.

No spin. No posturing. Just shared reality.

Within six months, those meetings transformed an adversarial police-services division into a functioning partnership.

Instead of grievances, we had spreadsheets and conversations about how to fix what the numbers revealed.

It's not magic; it's method.

People trust what they help analyze.

LRD360° Insight: Transparency doesn't weaken management; it immunizes it against rumor.

The Leadership Advantage

Leaders who last in unionized environments don't fight the current. They learn to steer it.

The first rule is understanding that unions don't exist in spite of management; they exist because of it.

When employees lose faith in the fairness of leadership systems, they organize to create one.

So, the question for every executive should never be, "How do we get rid of the union?"

It should be, "What conditions created it, and what can we learn from them?"

Those answers form the blueprint for sustainable leadership:

- Consistent communication prevents misinformation.
- Shared data builds credibility.
- Joint problem-solving creates ownership on both sides.

LRD360° Insight: Partnership is not surrender; it's strategy at scale.

Seeing the Union as a System, Not an Enemy

Every labor organization is a reflection of the workforce it represents. The mirror management doesn't always want to look into.

Behind every demand is data.

Behind every grievance is a pattern.

When a Chief Strategist learns to read those signals, the union stops being the opposition and becomes a diagnostic tool.

It's the ultimate employee engagement survey, except this one shows up prepared, passionate, and organized.

The LRD360° approach reframes collective bargaining as collective intelligence.

The table isn't a battlefield; it's a boardroom of lived experience.

The smartest leaders know that what the union brings isn't just pressure; it brings perspective.

LRD360° Insight: The union is the organization's most honest mirror. Ignore the reflection, and you'll trip over the cracks.

Partnership in Practice

At one point, I worked with a public-sector department that viewed its union purely as an obstacle.

Every grievance was "frivolous."

Every demand was "budget-busting."

After months of standoffs, morale collapsed — and so did performance.

Employees "worked to rule" (we'll discuss that in a later chapter).

When I stepped in, my first question to leadership wasn't, "What's wrong with the union?"

It was, "What's happening in your own ranks?"

The truth surfaced fast: Policies were applied inconsistently, communication was one-way, and trust was a casualty of ego.

We flipped the dynamic.

We created joint labor-management committees, co-chaired by supervisors and stewards.

We published transparent updates, shared staffing data, and invited union leaders into discussions about safety and scheduling.

The result?

Grievances dropped by half within a year.

Productivity went up.

Overtime costs went down.

Not because the contracts changed but because the conversations did.

That's what real partnership looks like.

Every petition is the echo of a missed conversation.

The LRD360° Strategy reframes that echo into evidence: proof that listening is the most cost-effective intervention any leader can make.

Closing Reflection: From Petition to Partnership

By the end of that year, the same HR department that once filed for representation now led quarterly joint training on trust and transparency.

The petition that once felt like a rebellion had become the foundation for reform.

That's the paradox of leadership: The feedback that stings the most is usually the feedback you needed first.

Unionization isn't the end of control. It's the beginning of accountability.

When leaders treat representation as dialogue rather than defeat, the table becomes what it was always meant to be, a space for shared truth.

LRD360° Insight: When leadership listens without defense, labor responds without defiance.

The next chapter takes us to the bargaining table itself, where posture meets principle and emotion meets evidence.

It's where all the lessons of leadership, trust, and transparency collide in real time.

Because once people organize, the next battle isn't in the street; it's across the table.

CHAPTER 3

The Table
The Blueprint of Negotiation

Where Structure Shapes Strategy Before a Word is Spoken

Once people organize, the next battle isn't in the street; it happens across the table.

Because the table is where movements mature or unravel.

It's where emotion meets execution, where strategy replaces slogans.

It's where both sides learn whether power can coexist with respect.

Some see the table as a battlefield.

Others see it as a bridge.

The truth is, it's both, depending on who walks in and why.

But the table doesn't exist in isolation. Around it lies the room, the theater of power where optics and perception set the tone long before a single clause is read.

The Room: Power and Optics

Every negotiation begins with a fragile calm.

The chairs are perfectly aligned, the microphones idle, the air conditioning hums with bureaucratic precision.

Laptops blink to life, coffee cups steam, and yet there's a weight in the room no one can quite name.

It's the awareness that every seat holds a story: a paycheck, a grievance, a policy, a promise.

The table itself is neutral only in appearance.

Its shape and distance silently decide the first balance of power.

Two feet too close and tempers flare; two feet too far and connection fades.

Even lighting matters. Glare breeds tension. Warmth builds focus.

Power often enters before people do.

You can feel it in how chairs are claimed.

The chief spokesperson's seat anchors one end; their counterpart mirrors them across the divide.

Counsel flank like sentinels, notebooks open, eyes scanning for advantage.

Observers line the back wall, silent but deliberate, representing the invisible constituencies who aren't in the room but will live with its decisions.

Optics matter.

The union may arrive in matching jackets as a visible show of solidarity.

Management may arrive in coordinated suits as a signal of discipline and unity.

Both sides read the other's staging like poker tells.

A single shifted chair can reset hierarchy.

The calm before the first word isn't peace; it's pressure suspended.

Everyone is watching everyone else.

The note-taker adjusts a laptop lid. Nervousness or control?

A lawyer flips through the binder. Stalling or asserting?

Even the placement of pens can betray psychology.

At a seasoned table, this choreography of optics is studied as carefully as any proposal.

LRD360° Insight: The room negotiates before the people do. Respect starts with how you enter the space.

The first exchange often isn't verbal at all.

It's eye contact.

The nod of acknowledgment.

The pause before anyone says good morning.

And in that moment, the experienced negotiator reads everything: who's defensive, who's overconfident, who's waiting to challenge authority.

This is where discipline matters most.

The chief spokesperson's tone, body language, and pacing dictate the room's emotional bandwidth.

A calm entrance communicates readiness.

A hurried one communicates reaction.

The room, like a living organism, adapts to whichever energy it's fed.

For all the emphasis on preparation, few leaders train for optics.

Yet optics are the unspoken architecture of trust.

Before a single clause is debated, posture and tone either build a foundation for collaboration or a wall of suspicion.

That's why great teams treat the table as both stage and mirror: a stage because everything is seen, a mirror because everything you project returns to you.

The Rhythm: Process and Posture

Before the first proposal slides across the polished surface, the real work has already been done or neglected.

What the public sees as negotiation is only the performance; the rehearsal happens quietly, in late-night calls, data runs, and pre-briefs that build muscle memory.

The table merely exposes the discipline behind the preparation.

The First Sound

The first sound in any negotiation isn't a voice. It's the shuffle of papers and the click of a pen.

Those small sounds signal readiness or reveal hesitation.

A Chief Strategist knows how to read them.

You can tell when a union team walks in unified: folders aligned, eyes forward, chairs pulled close together.

You can also tell when management has spent the morning calming nerves instead of refining counterproposals.

Every detail is a tell.

Seasoned leaders hear tempo before they hear tone.

Union's Posture

When the union takes its seat, posture is power. Shoulders square, stewards stacked in formation, the Chief Spokesperson at the head: a visual declaration of solidarity.

Their energy speaks first.

If they lean in, they're ready to work.

If they recline, arms crossed, the first day will be theatre.

The best Chief Strategists respect that energy but refuse to mirror it. Calm becomes the counterweight that steadies chaos.

Management's Counterbalance

On the management side, preparation means walking in with both data and demeanor.

Numbers win arguments, but tone wins trust.

You don't meet emotion with emotion; you meet it with rhythm.

You anticipate the opening volley, but you control the tempo.

Too fast and it feels like dismissal; too slow and it feels like stalling.

Mastery at the table is tempo management: knowing when to accelerate, when to pause, and when silence does the work for you.

The Dance Begins

This is where bargaining becomes choreography.

Offers, counters, and caucuses unfold in a rhythm that can feel almost musical when done right.

There's a point when everyone in the room starts moving to the same unheard beat, even opponents.

That's when you know the table is alive.

Each side tests boundaries, each word chosen to move the room one inch closer to agreement.

At its best, negotiation becomes conversation with consequence.

When Tensions Rise

But the music can shift without warning.

One misplaced phrase; one ill-timed laugh; and the rhythm fractures.

Suddenly, whispers turn into walkouts.

Emotions rise because everyone at the table believes they're defending something bigger than themselves: dignity, fairness, legacy.

The Chief Strategist must hold the center, reading not just words but breathing patterns, body shifts, and tone.

When tension climbs, silence is the strongest instrument.

Composure is leadership's metronome.

The Pivot

Every bargaining table has a pivot. That exact moment when the energy changes direction.

Sometimes it's a data point that lands perfectly; sometimes it's a story that humanizes a sterile spreadsheet.

The pivot isn't luck; it's presence.

You have to feel it coming before it arrives.

A good strategist doesn't just steer arguments; they steer emotion.

And when you find that inflection, don't announce it. You anchor it.

The Internal Dialogue

While the room debates, the strategist's mind never stops mapping:

What's next? Who hasn't spoken? Who's signaling fatigue? What are we not hearing?

The internal dialogue is constant.

You're decoding every cue, a raised eyebrow, a shifted chair, because negotiation isn't just about what's said aloud.

It's a living language of pressure and patience.

Rebuild and Recalibrate

Once the first session ends, every strategist debriefs the team: not to relive the meeting, but to rebuild understanding.

Who showed leadership? Who lost focus? Which proposal resonated, which stalled?

The post-session analysis is the most honest mirror.

This is where you realign the team before the next day's battle.

Momentum, once lost, takes twice the effort to rebuild.

Reflection is rehearsal for the next round.

LRD360° Insight: Preparation isn't paperwork. It's people work: aligning minds before the first word is spoken.

The Tone: Trust, Tension, and Command Presence

Every table eventually stops being about proposals and starts being about people.

By the midpoint of bargaining, the spreadsheets blur together, and what remains are the intangibles: how voices sound, how long silences last, and how each person reacts when they feel misunderstood.

This is the psychological table — the terrain where control depends less on logic and more on emotional fluency.

Here, the Chief Strategist becomes less an advocate and more a field commander, reading terrain, not text.

Tone Sets Trajectory

Tone is the first thing people feel and the last thing they remember.

A Chief Strategist doesn't just listen for what is said, but how it lands.

A clipped response can erase hours of progress; a measured one can rebuild a bridge that almost burned.

In tense sessions, tone must do what words can't: soothe the room without surrendering ground.

Tone is the soft skill that makes hard power work.

When tempers flare, calm becomes the loudest voice.

LRD360° Insight: The strongest negotiator in the room isn't the loudest. It's the one who can lower the volume without losing authority.

Trust as Currency

Data builds arguments, but trust builds agreements.

Each side arrives with its own doubts, and every misstep (a delayed answer, a changed draft, a misquoted clause) withdraws from that invisible trust account.

Leaders who understand this treat every interaction as a deposit.

Transparency, consistency, and follow-through are worth more than any clever phrase.

The best tables aren't won; they're trusted into being.

Trust is the compound interest of leadership: slow to earn, quick to spend, and impossible to fake.

Tension as Energy

Tension isn't the problem. It's energy waiting to be channeled.

It shows people still care enough to fight for what matters.

The mistake is letting that energy control the room instead of channeling it.

A seasoned strategist uses tension the way a conductor uses crescendos: to heighten focus, not chaos.

Let frustration crest, then redirect it toward problem-solving.

Call a caucus a private meeting where a party or faction discusses strategy and aligns positions before returning to the full session, not to escape, but to reset.

Invite the other side back not with new numbers, but with renewed perspective.

LRD360° Insight: You can't eliminate tension; you can only decide who it serves.

Command Presence and the KLE Principle

Military leaders call it Key Leader Engagement (KLE): the discipline of entering a high-stakes room with calm authority, emotional awareness, and precise intent.

It's not about rank; it's about presence.

The same principle applies at the bargaining table.

When the strategist enters, every movement, tone, and gesture sets the emotional perimeter.

A steady posture stabilizes the room; a reactive tone destabilizes it.

Whether in combat zones or conference rooms, the mission is the same: maintain composure, build rapport, and secure trust through respect.

That's the unseen skill: the ability to command attention without demanding it.

True presence doesn't shout; it steadies.

And when that steadiness fills a room, strategy can finally breathe.

The Mirror Moment

At some point, both sides hit a mirror moment. They realize the conflict isn't between them, but within them.

Union teams must decide whether they're bargaining for progress or payback.

Management must ask whether they're defending the budget or their pride.

The strategist's task is to guide the room through that reflection without shame, to remind both sides what the mission really is.

That moment of shared clarity can shift weeks of stalemate.

The Rebuild

When sessions get personal, rebuilding trust requires humility and timing.

A quiet apology for tone, an acknowledgment of shared fatigue, or even a small concession on a symbolic issue can restore balance.

You don't repair relationships with grand gestures. You repair them with respect made visible.

Every act of patience becomes a structural beam in the rebuilding of trust.

LRD360° Insight: When tension rises, don't match heat with heat. Lower the temperature and raise the trust.

The Strategy: Momentum, Closure, and Leadership Reflection

By the final stretch of bargaining, every participant feels the miles.

What began as postures and positions has become something quieter: rhythm, fatigue, instinct.

This is where strategy shifts from offense to orchestration.

You're no longer proving your case; you're protecting the integrity of the process itself.

Momentum as Leverage

Momentum is the invisible currency of bargaining.

Once a deal begins to take shape, each small agreement accelerates the next.

A wise Chief Strategist knows when to lock in that pace and when to pause for recalibration.

Too much speed, and people feel rushed.

Too little, and doubt creeps in.

Momentum isn't motion; it's belief. When people believe progress is possible, they start to move with you instead of against you.

LRD360° Insight: Momentum feeds trust; trust fuels closure.

The Meaning Behind the Terms

By now, every clause on the table has a story attached.

A steward's insistence on break language might trace back to a single bad shift.

A manager's push for clearer attendance rules might stem from one incident that spiraled.

This is where empathy meets execution.

Great strategists read between the lines; they translate pain into policy.

If you reduce every issue to dollars or data, you'll miss the meaning that sustains compliance.

The best negotiators codify humanity without compromising structure.

The Strategy of Silence

When negotiations near closure, silence becomes your sharpest instrument.

The other side will fill it with nervous chatter, late-hour appeals, or last-minute asks.

Let them.

A steady quiet communicates confidence.

It signals that the table has already spoken; now it's time to listen.

In those final stretches, every unnecessary word can reopen an issue thought to be settled.

Discipline wins deals more often than persuasion.

Managing Fatigue

End-stage bargaining runs on caffeine and willpower.

After twelve-hour days, clarity blurs.

Tempers rise not from ideology but exhaustion.

The strategist's role here is part guardian, part tactician: Know when to push for tentative agreements and when to step back before a misstep becomes a mistake.

Fatigue turns ego into error. Protect the people before the paper.

Closure with Integrity

When the final draft sits between both sides, the instinct is celebration and relief.

But closure deserves precision.

Read every word again, out loud if you must.

Confirm intent. Confirm numbers. Confirm dignity.

Because tomorrow, interpretation begins, and how you close determines whether implementation will be smooth or chaotic.

True closure isn't ink on paper; it's mutual understanding.

It's two sides leaving with different outcomes but shared respect.

It's the silent handshake after the signatures fade.

The contract ends the negotiation; integrity begins the relationship.

LRD360° Insight: A deal's strength is measured not by what it wins, but by how it ends.

Closing Reflection

When the room finally empties, what remains is the echo of what was said, restrained, and revealed.

That silence is diagnostic. It shows whether you led with control or with ego, with clarity or with pride.

In the military, **commanders** hold after-action reflections, not to assign blame, but to strengthen discipline **and morale.**

The same applies at the negotiation table: Reflection isn't about replaying the conflict; it's about refining your composure.

Leadership isn't about victory; it's about stewardship.

Understanding that every agreement becomes the foundation for the next.

And everyone who sat across from you will remember whether they left with dignity.

Mastery isn't found in clauses or closing **arguments,** but in how you carry the room once the talking stops.

Because the table always remembers tone longer than terms.

CHAPTER 4

Labor Pains
The Delivery of a Deal

Where Pressure Tightens and Every Move Feels Measured

After giving birth to four children and more collective bargaining agreements than I can count, I've learned that bargaining and childbirth share the same rhythm of anticipation, endurance, and release.

I've labored through both: eight hours with my son, thirty-six minutes with my daughter, and contract sessions that stretched thirty-two hours straight.

Each follows the same pattern: early optimism, mid-stage exhaustion, and a final push that tests every ounce of discipline and faith you have left.

So, when I say labor pains, I mean both kinds, because every agreement that changes lives is born through struggle, and every leader who's been through it recognizes the contractions long before the delivery.

The bargaining table never really closes. Each agreement leaves traces of tension and trust that carry into the next cycle: echoes of lessons unlearned and promises renewed. Negotiation, like labor, always returns: different faces, same contractions. The next round begins not with a gavel but a heartbeat.

Like every birth, it starts quietly, with anticipation disguised as readiness. Both sides believe they know what's coming. Neither does.

Trimester One: Conception and Confrontation

Every negotiation begins with the same uneasy excitement as a first trimester, full of anticipation, anxiety, and the illusion of control.

Everyone believes they're ready.

No one really is.

Both sides arrive armed with their versions of righteousness.

Management wants stability and fiscal discipline.

The union wants recognition and reward.

Somewhere in between sits the impossible: an agreement that satisfies both.

But this stage isn't about substance yet; it's about tone.

The first trimester determines the emotional architecture of everything that follows. How tension is managed, how respect is measured, how power behaves when first tested.

The early sessions at the bargaining table establish the rhythm: how fast the table moves, who dominates the dialogue, who retreats when pressure builds.

The first trimester is full of surface calm and hidden nausea, the kind leaders learn to mask so no one sees the strain beneath the smile.

Even when the conversation sounds professional, both sides are secretly watching body language (the raised eyebrow, the sideways glance, the exaggerated sigh).

These small tells reveal what position papers never will: who's nervous, who's confident, and who's bluffing.

Preparation is the prenatal care of bargaining.

This is when leaders test their internal alliances.

- Are the department heads aligned?
- Are the talking points consistent?
- Has anyone rehearsed what not to say?

Most failures are conceived here, not at the bargaining table, but in the prep room before it.

LRD360° Insight: Negotiations rarely collapse over one bad session; they collapse because no one corrected the tone of the first one.

The conception stage is about message discipline, not control but coherence.

The smartest negotiators don't try to win the opening; they try to learn the room.

They listen for hesitations, read who whispers to whom, and note who's taking the most notes.

These quiet cues become tomorrow's strategy.

At this point, adrenaline masquerades as confidence.

Everyone believes they're the calmest person in the room until the first proposal hits the table and the air shifts.

The smallest question "How did you arrive at that number?" suddenly sounds like a challenge.

In the early trimester, tone is everything.

The way a negotiator responds to that first question writes the emotional script for the rest of the contract.

A defensive answer invites escalation.

A composed answer buys time.

The best strategists build relationships in these openings.

They look for small human exchanges: shared humor, acknowledgment of hard work, even mutual fatigue.

These are the handholds that prevent the climb from collapsing later.

There's also a quiet art to pacing.

Too much progress too fast breeds suspicion; too little breeds resentment.

The first trimester is about calibration. Discovering how far you can go without losing trust.

And like any first stage of labor, there are warning signs:

- Unplanned sidebars between team members.
- A sudden change in who does the talking.
- Repeated clarifications that really mean "We're not ready."
- Early signs of a disrupter (covered in the next chapter).

A skilled leader reads these moments without panic.

They steady their breathing, slow the conversation, and remind everyone often gently that the goal is progress, not punishment.

Because at this stage, no contract will be born, but every tone will.

LRD360° Insight: The first words spoken at a bargaining table are like a heartbeat on a monitor. Ignore the rhythm and you'll miss the warning.

By the time this trimester closes, the foundation is either firm or fractured.

And then the rhythm changes. The early optimism fades, the tone sharpens, and both sides begin to feel the weight of what they've conceived.

Trimester Two: Pressure, Pain & Pivots

By the second trimester, the pregnancy is showing — and so are the cracks at the bargaining table.

What began with optimism now shows the strain of repetition: the same arguments, the same frustrations, the same unspoken fatigue.

The easy topics are done, the posturing is old, and every session feels like déjà vu.

The bargaining table now has rhythm, but rhythm isn't harmony.

It's the repetition of strain.

Every side has its mantra:

"The budget can't absorb that."

"Our members won't accept less."

The words change slightly each week, but the melody stays the same.

This is where leadership either matures or mutates.

Pressure reshapes tone.

Even professionals who begin calm, can harden under repetition.

A stray comment from an outside observer (a rumor of what another union got, a headline about executive pay) can undo weeks of trust-building.

LRD360° Insight: Negotiation is never just between two sides. It's between two rooms of competing expectations.

Here, the Chief Strategist earns their title.

This stage isn't about offering more; it's about re-anchoring the dialogue.

When numbers collide, emotion follows.

A good strategist doesn't fight emotion head-on; they redirect it.

They translate outrage into questions:

"What does respect look like for your members?"

"If not 10%, what problem are you trying to solve with 10%?"

Every proposal carries a story.

When people say, "We need more," they mean, "We feel unseen." The strategist listens for that invisible sentence. The meaning behind the words.

The second trimester is also where fatigue sets in, physical, emotional, and political.

Bargaining teams start keeping score internally:

- Who's doing the talking?
- Who's giving in too fast?
- Who keeps calling a sidebar?

A sidebar is a private huddle between the principal and the chief spokesperson, the bargaining equivalent of a coach calling a time-out to recalibrate the next play.

Teams start keeping quiet audits: mental scorecards of who's leading, who's yielding, and who's losing patience.

These silent tallies can fracture even the best-run teams. That's when the strategist must lead inwardly, not just across the table.

Sometimes the pressure isn't from the union or management — it's from silence above.

Boards and executives, who applauded collaboration at the start, grow impatient.

"What's taking so long?" they ask, forgetting that negotiation is deliberate by design.

Leaders must shield the process from panic.

And this is when pivots happen.

A pivot isn't surrender; it's strategy.

It's the art of reframing without retreating.

Instead of defending why a proposal can't be done, you ask what problem it's meant to fix.

Instead of saying No, you say, Let's see if we can get there differently.

That pivot restores motion.

Without it, the table stalls; stalled tables invite outside intervention.

When sides stop talking, others start.

The media, influencers, even other unions fill the void.

In the middle trimester, communication is oxygen.

Lose it, and the process suffocates.

That's why leaders must double down on transparency, not in public press releases, but in private check-ins with their own teams.

This is the trimester when whispers become threats:

"Maybe we should just strike."

"Maybe they need to feel pressure."

"Maybe it's time for a walkout."

The best leaders listen without flinching.

These whispers are contractions. They signal what's coming, not what must come.

LRD360° Insight: A strike doesn't start with picket signs; it starts with someone feeling unheard.

And so, the strategist begins the pivot from bargaining to stabilizing, protecting relationships even as rhetoric rises.

They introduce breathing room: a side meeting, a break for data verification, or a small win both sides can celebrate.

This stage is where emotional intelligence separates leaders from negotiators.

You can't out-logic fatigue; you out-lead it.

By now, the sides know each other too well. The jokes, the sarcasm, the faces of frustration.

There's no mystery left, only management.

That's when trust becomes currency.

Because the second trimester always ends the same way: Everyone is tired, but no one can stop.

The deal isn't ready, but the process can't pause.

And deep down, both sides sense that something is about to change, that pressure will either fracture trust or deliver a breakthrough.

The contractions begin — not of body, but of belief. Every assumption tightens. Every sentence feels like strain. What began as dialogue now becomes endurance.

By the third trimester, every conversation feels like labor.

Everyone's swollen with frustration, and the bargaining table that once symbolized diplomacy now feels like confinement.

The finish line is close enough to see, but not close enough to touch.

The room sounds different now.

Gone are the long monologues and polite recitations of proposals.

The words are sharper.

The pauses heavier.

People start to lean in, cross their arms, and breathe audibly through irritation.

These are contractions. The natural tightening that signals something's about to give.

This is where strategy becomes endurance.

All the talk about partnership starts to fade, replaced by survival instincts.

Leaders count to ten before responding.

Legal counselors look down at their papers to keep from making eye contact.

Every exchange feels like it could be the one that blows up the deal.

LRD360° Insight: The closer you get to resolution, the more fragile it becomes. Tension peaks just before release.

At this stage, truth starts leaking out in unguarded ways.

Someone sighs too deeply, a muttered "We're done with this," a chair scrapes back too fast.

These are signals of strain beneath the surface, emotional microfractures that precede rupture.

The seasoned strategist listens differently now — not for what's said, but for what's no longer being said.

Silence becomes diagnostic.

When crisis hits, it's rarely dramatic.

It's subtle: a raised voice, a walkout, a sarcastic remark that lands wrong.

Suddenly, the air changes.

Everyone's guard rises, the lawyers start rechecking notes, and someone inevitably says, "We need a break."

Here's where leaders earn their credibility: how they handle the break.

Do they vent in front of their team, feeding frustration?

Or do they debrief calmly, reframing emotion into insight?

A veteran negotiator knows this is the point where deals die or are born.

The break is the breathing room before the final push.

LRD360° Insight: Crisis is neutral. What you do next decides whether it's collapse or clarity.

Sometimes, the crisis comes from outside: a board member leaks a number, a rumor spreads on social media, or an employee post goes viral mid-bargain.

When that happens, you can't chase perception; you must return to principle.

The strategist becomes the stabilizer with the steady tone, no reactionary statements, and only clarity.

The third trimester is about delivery — not of demands, but of discipline.

Here, the sides begin trading their final lists.

The air is heavy with trade-offs.

"What are you willing to live without?" becomes the unspoken refrain on both sides.

And then, finally, the words everyone has been waiting for:

"We can work with that."

It doesn't sound like triumph.

It sounds like relief.

Because in labor, and in bargaining, no one leaves untouched.

Everyone gives something.

Everyone carries something.

When the contract is finally printed, it feels less like victory and more like survival.

Both sides stare at the signature lines longer than they'll admit.

Because signing isn't just a formality; it's surrender to what's been birthed: a new relationship that will now live or die by how the next months unfold.

That's why the best leaders stay humble in that moment.

They know the celebration will be short-lived.

The postpartum phase, the implementation, the interpretation, the training, will determine whether the child they just delivered thrives or becomes a problem child no one wants to claim.

And so, as the papers are stacked, the tension subsides, replaced by a strange quiet.

The sound of pens clicking feels ceremonial.

People gather their folders, shake hands, and exhale for the first time in weeks.

It's over … or so they think.

LRD360° Insight: Bargaining doesn't end with signatures; it ends when behavior aligns with what was signed.

But every leader knows delivery isn't the end of labor. The most challenging work comes after, when exhaustion meets expectation and the real healing begins.

Because once the room empties, the next phase begins: the recovery, the reflection, the rebuilding of trust that got stretched thin in the process.

That's the postpartum of negotiation; the part most people skip, but leaders never do.

Postpartum: Healing the Table and the Team

When the room finally clears, the quiet feels foreign. The bargaining table itself seems bruised, not from impact, but from the weight of what it held.

And as that weight lifts, the next phase begins: the recovery, the reflection, the rebuilding of trust.

The echoes of argument still hang in the air like the memory of contractions.

What was once strategy and survival becomes reflection.

The deal is signed, but the people are frayed.

In every negotiation, there is a postpartum stage, the period no one warns you about.

The adrenaline fades, the smiles feel stiff, and reality creeps in: You still have to live with one another.

This is where leadership reemerges, stripped of microphones and megaphones.

The strategist's voice softens; the communicator's tone changes.

The work now is to rehumanize the process that bargaining dehumanized.

The Emotional Recovery

The first few days after a deal are like the first days after surgery, relief mixed with soreness.

Employees who fought for months to be heard now wonder if it was worth it.

Supervisors who spent weeks defending the company's position feel defensive about their own reputations.

Everyone walks through hallways quietly, pretending to be fine.

LRD360° Insight: The most dangerous silence in any organization comes right after a contract is signed.

This is the moment for calm visibility — not speeches, but presence.

A leader who stops by a department, acknowledges the effort, or simply says, "We're moving forward together," can reset morale faster than any memo.

The Practical Recovery

Then comes the translation. Every clause must now become policy.

Departments begin asking, "What does this mean for us?" That's where the unseen tension hides — not in the clauses themselves, but in how people read and interpret them.

Implementation memos, manager trainings, and FAQs are the stitches that hold the organization together. Skip them, and small misunderstandings become reopened wounds.

The Chief Strategist must coordinate this phase like an after-action review: collecting the lessons without reopening the arguments. The smartest teams send two messages at once: gratitude for collaboration and clarity about execution.

The Relationship Reset

For all the talk of "sides," the truth is everyone works in the same building.

The cafeteria doesn't have a management section and a union section.

That's why this stage requires humility.

No victory laps.

No "We showed them."

Reconciliation starts with tone.

The same leaders who argued across the table must now model partnership in public.

If they fail to, the workforce will mirror their tension.

If they succeed, even skeptics begin to relax.

LRD360° Insight: You don't rebuild trust with policy; you rebuild it with posture.

Some leaders underestimate how visible they are right after a deal.

A single eye-roll during a post-ratification meeting can reignite the flame.

Every gesture either confirms unity or reopens the divide.

The Strategic Debrief

Once the emotional fog lifts, the strategist must dissect the entire experience:

- What worked?
- What broke?

- What surprised?
- Who carried influence?
- Who lost credibility?

Which arguments landed, and which triggered defense?

This internal review shouldn't be punitive — it should be developmental.

The goal is not to assign blame but to refine muscle memory.

Bargaining is cyclical; what you learn in this recovery defines the next conception.

Some organizations schedule a post-bargaining symposium.

Others use informal lunches or retreats.

The format doesn't matter; the reflection does.

The Long Game

The best leaders don't treat ratification as an ending; they treat it as recalibration.

They begin the next contract the next day — not by drafting proposals, but by managing relationships: keeping promises, solving grievances, recognizing effort, maintaining dignity.

It's tempting to move on quickly, to dive back into regular business.

But unprocessed conflict doesn't fade; it ferments.

That's why the postpartum stage is not optional.

It's maintenance for the human infrastructure that keeps everything running.

LRD360° Insight: You can't heal what you rush past.

When handled right, this phase produces something rare: resilience.

The workforce becomes more resilient.

Management becomes more empathetic.

And the next round begins on higher ground.

Leadership, at its core, is less about delivering the deal than sustaining the peace that makes future deals possible.

And so the strategist closes the binder, not with pride, but with perspective.

The next table awaits: new faces, new numbers, same principles.

Closing Reflection

Negotiation, like labor, is the art of endurance: a process of contraction, discomfort, and eventual creation.

Each session delivers something new: sometimes an agreement, sometimes a lesson. What matters most is whether the experience strengthens the institution or merely exhausts it.

LRD360° Insight: Leadership isn't measured by how long the labor lasted, but by what was born from it.

When Labor Meets Sabotage

But not every pregnancy is free of complications.

Some begin with promise and progress, only to be tested by forces that never wanted the birth to succeed.

In negotiation, those complications have names, faces, and motives.

Most pregnancies end with relief: a healthy delivery, even if marked by pain.

But not all labor is that merciful.

Some negotiations begin with promise and descend into chaos, not because of disagreement, but because of disruption at the bargaining table.

Every Chief Strategist eventually meets the outlier, the person who arrives not to build but to break, whose purpose is to ensure the baby doesn't survive.

CHAPTER 5

Bullying
The Disrupter at the Table

Where Ego Enters Loudly and Logic Leaves Quietly

The first session should always set the tone for a season of collaboration: a cautious dance where respect frames every move.

But sometimes, from the very first moment, you can feel the difference.

Not every pregnancy ends in a smooth delivery; some are interrupted by hands that were never meant to help.

It's there in the way the opposing Chief Spokesperson (CSP) walks in — not with purpose, but with provocation.

His team follows like a platoon marching into battle, not into a room meant for problem-solving.

Before introductions are done, he drops the word strike into the air like a grenade.

The word hangs there, heavy, unnecessary, meant to draw blood before the first proposal hits the table.

This was one of our largest bargaining units, nearly three thousand employees under one roof.

And from that very first day, it was clear their chief spokesperson wasn't here to negotiate.

He was here to fight.

You could feel it in the air: the kind of tension that doesn't build; it arrives.

Everyone at that table knew it.

My team of seven sat across from an army dressed in unity.

Their leader's tone wasn't just firm; it was designed to provoke.

Every statement was a dare.

Every pause, a performance.

In bargaining, respect is the table's currency.

Once it's gone, the process bankrupts itself.

And sometimes, that loss of respect isn't accidental — it's engineered.

There are strategists who don't come to the table to solve problems.

They come to set fires.

The Disrupter

There are times when one side enters not to resolve, but to rupture — to force chaos and call it victory.

These are the disrupters.

They masquerade as negotiators, but their strategy is built on emotional manipulation.

A disrupter's goal isn't a fair deal; it's spectacle.

They thrive on division, between managers and staff, between leadership and membership, between truth and rumor.

They exaggerate, distort, and weaponize every misstep.

They present themselves as saviors of the people while quietly engineering the conflict they'll later claim to cure.

In this particular case, the disrupter was good.

Too good.

From day one, his tone said: We're not here to talk; we're here to take.

He mocked proposals, compared management to oppressive regimes, and labeled me Justice Scalia. A deliberate move, crafted to paint me as inflexible, biased, and out of touch.

I'd been in enough rooms to know when words were chosen to spark rage, not results.

That's the disrupter's craft: using emotion as a weapon.

To rally employees into leaving their paychecks behind, you have to convince them they're fighting for survival.

And that's exactly what a disrupter does.

They create an us-versus-them narrative so powerful it replaces reason.

Every management proposal becomes proof of oppression.

Every attempt at compromise becomes betrayal.

They convince workers that every denial, delay, or data point is an act of disrespect.

Once the room internalizes that, logic leaves, and survival takes over.

The disrupter's proposals are always the same: lofty, emotional, and mathematically impossible.

- Fifteen percent wage increases "to match the struggle."

- Automatic promotions "for loyalty."

- Daily self-assignment of shifts "to ensure fairness."

None of these are designed to pass.

They're designed to provoke rejection.

Because rejection fuels outrage — and outrage fuels action.

LRD360° Insight: A strike doesn't start with a picket sign. It starts with the erosion of respect.

The Spark

By the second session, you can already feel the shift.

Stewards who once nodded in quiet acknowledgment now fold their arms.

Managers who once shared jokes in the hallway are met with silence.

Smiles disappear.

The tension between the sides becomes visible. Physical.

You are now the enemy.

The one standing between them and equality, value, and, more importantly, dignity.

Even the scheduling of sessions becomes tactical.

The disrupter starts clustering them closer to the contract's expiration date, tightening the window so every delay feels like betrayal.

This way, when the clock runs out, he can point and say, "See? They don't care about you. They want this to expire."

And when that happens, the table's no longer a forum.

It's a fuse.

By the third session, it's no longer a negotiation — it's a show.

Every comment from management becomes a headline in waiting.

Every counterproposal is twisted into a rallying cry.

The disrupter doesn't seek movement; he seeks momentum.

The louder the conflict, the stronger his control over the room.

That's the thing about disrupters — they don't want members to think; they want them to feel.

Anger is easier to lead than logic.

At this point, the bargaining room transforms from a table of strategy into a stage of performance.

The union members arrive in coordinated shirts and jackets, slogans on the front, solidarity on the back.

They don't make eye contact anymore.

The small talk that used to fill quiet moments, "How's your daughter?" or "How was the weekend?", vanishes.

It's replaced by a wall of silence, the kind that doesn't just divide the room but suffocates it.

And in that silence, the disrupter thrives.

He speaks loudly enough for the hallway to hear, making sure his words ripple through the membership waiting outside.

"They don't respect you."
"They think you're replaceable."
"They're pocketing bonuses while you fight for crumbs."

These words sting not because they're true — but because they could be true in a world without trust.

They're already pre-loaded in bargaining updates, primed to incite action.

Preparation Meets Provocation: The Shift to Defense

When faced with a disrupter, the role of a Chief Strategist changes overnight.

You're no longer building a bridge; you're fortifying the walls.

The moment you recognize the game, that this isn't about wages or work rules but about chaos, your priority shifts to continuity.

You move from bargaining strategy to business continuity.

You secure operations, anticipate disruption, and prepare departments for impact.

You plan for turbulence you didn't create but must now navigate.

Preparation becomes power when the other side mistakes noise for negotiation.

Recognizing the Signs of a Disrupter

Disruption isn't random; it's a formula.

And once you learn to read it, you stop being surprised by the storm.

There are always clues.

A seasoned negotiator can feel the storm before the lightning.

- Language that burns bridges. The disrupter's vocabulary is built on accusation. Words like exploitation, corruption, and injustice dominate his speech, regardless of the proposal's content.

- Inflated proposals. Fifteen-percent wage increases, automatic promotions, or full employee control over scheduling — the math is never meant to work. The goal is rejection, to stoke outrage when management inevitably says no.

- Manufactured deadlines. Sessions are scheduled closer to the contract's expiration, forcing the employer into perceived delay, a tactic that paints leadership as dismissive or unprepared.

- Public theater. Union newsletters and social media posts become propaganda tools, each update edited for outrage instead of accuracy.

- Loss of connection. The personal relationships that once sustained trust vanish. Managers become "the enemy." Even casual hallway greetings are met with suspicion.

- Mocking reason, rewarding outrage. In their world, defiance equals dignity.

Once these signs appear, you're no longer at a table of negotiation — you're standing at the edge of a strike line waiting to be drawn.

LRD360° Insight: Some strikes are not born of unmet needs. It's provoked. It happens when a disrupter, under the guise of representing workers, decides the path to relevance runs through chaos.

Composure as Counter-Strategy

A disrupter thrives on spectacle.

Their strategy depends on provoking emotion, not resolution.

The moment a CSP responds in kind, the disrupter wins twice: once in the room, and again in perception.

A seasoned strategist knows the strength of non-participation.

They don't meet volume with volume; they let professionalism do the talking.

When tension peaks, they quietly reframe the moment:

"You've seen me at this table before. Does this feel like progress toward a deal — or toward a fight?"

That single question pierces rhetoric and forces reflection.

It reframes the room without accusation, giving everyone a moment to recognize manipulation for what it is.

Real strength is rarely loud.

It's in the poise that can't be provoked, the steadiness that refuses to mirror chaos.

The CSP who maintains composure turns the disrupter's aggression into its own undoing.

LRD360° Insight: When you hold your ground in silence, the noise eventually unmasks itself.

When Words Turn into War

Then it happens.

- The contract expires.
- The disrupter's speeches have done their work.
- The membership votes — not necessarily for better wages, but for validation.
- The picket signs go up before dawn.
- The chants echo across the parking lot:
- "Respect us!"
- "Fair pay now!"
- "No justice, no peace!"
- Inside, departments scramble.

- Supervisors cover shifts.

HR fields calls from employees torn between solidarity and survival.

Some workers cross the line quietly, guilt heavy on their faces.

Others post pictures online, arms raised in pride.

As the strike begins, the disrupter smiles.

Because in that moment, he's achieved exactly what he wanted, chaos that looks like courage.

LRD360° Insight: A true leader builds a movement around principles. A disrupter builds one around pain and then feeds it.

Weeks of Smoke and Silence

The first few days always start with noise.

Picket signs line the entrances; bullhorns replace the morning coffee.

The press shows up, microphones out, searching for conflict.

But by day five, the noise fades and fatigue sets in.

The reality of lost paychecks and uncertainty hits everyone differently, the single parents counting grocery money, the nurses covering double shifts, the supervisors absorbing vitriol from both sides.

That's when leadership is tested.

Not when things are loud, but when they're quiet.

During one of the longest strikes in Illinois public-sector history, it looked like stalemate on the surface.

But beneath it was something more dangerous: emotional attrition.

The disrupter kept pushing messaging that made compromise impossible.

Every day without resolution was framed as "proof" that management didn't care.

Yet the longer it went, the more members began to see the gap between rhetoric and reality.

LRD360° Insight: By the time the strike begins, both sides have already lost something intangible: the ease of trust.

Business Continuity: Leadership Under Fire

Preparation was everything.

Before the strike even started, my team had executed a full business-continuity plan. We worked through the night: recalibrating schedules, mapping contingencies, and double-checking every line of defense. Coffee cups emptied as we built a plan robust enough that no critical service would fail by morning.

- Agency coverage was secured for critical services.

- Emergency protocols ensured that law-enforcement and healthcare operations never stopped.

- Legal counsel stood ready to file injunctions if essential services were compromised.

These weren't reactive measures — they were the result of reading the signs early.

When you recognize a disrupter at the table, your job shifts.

You're no longer just negotiating a contract; you're safeguarding the organization's mission.

Continuity planning isn't about breaking the union; it's about protecting everyone who depends on the work still being done, patients, residents, families, the public.

A strike might make headlines, but life can't stop because two sides lost their rhythm.

The Disrupter's Unraveling

By the second week, cracks begin to show.

The exaggerated promises — the "fifteen percent across-the-board raise," the "automatic upgrades" — no longer sound achievable.

Employees start asking questions the disrupter can't answer:

When will we get paid again?
What's the plan if they don't move?
How much is left in the strike fund?

The strike was supposed to be a statement of power. Instead, it became a spotlight, revealing who was leading, and why.

Many members quietly return to work, choosing stability over spectacle.

Other unions that had initially offered support stayed on the sidelines, unwilling to attach their reputations to a fight that had lost direction.

The disrupter had built his campaign on outrage, but outrage burns fast and leaves only exhaustion behind; especially when it's manufactured.

LRD360° Insight: Courage isn't proven in conflict; it's measured in how you rebuild afterward. Leadership isn't about winning the strike; it's about restoring the table.

Even union leaders should view strikes as extraordinary acts — remedies, not reflexes.

Each one leaves marks on morale, membership, and memory.

The true test of leadership lies not in rallying a crowd, but in leading them back home afterward.

After the Storm: Rebuilding Respect

When the strike ends and the posters come down, what's left isn't peace — it's pause.

No one knows quite what to say.

Employees return, some quietly proud, others quietly resentful.

Supervisors over-manage to prove control.

Leaders over-apologize to show empathy.

And in that uneasy middle sits the strategist, tasked with restoring balance without rewriting history.

The truth is, no contract heals immediately.

People carry what happened at the table into every hallway conversation, every staff meeting, every sideways glance.

The work of leadership becomes psychological: rebuilding trust in invisible increments.

The goal isn't to erase the storm. The goal is to prove the structure held.

That's what credibility looks like after conflict: The building still stands, even if the paint is cracked.

LRD360° Insight: You can't rebuild trust with memos. You rebuild it in moments that prove you mean what you said.

Rebuilding in Real Time

The morning after a strike feels deceptively calm.

The hallways are quieter, the chants gone — but their echo lingers.

For the employer, the job isn't to win the day after; it's to restore order and rebuild relationships.

For the union, it's to rebuild trust without surrendering credibility.

The air may seem still, but every conversation hums with residual tension.

If the union was successful, they return empowered, a victory lap of solidarity.

If the strike faltered, leadership must return humble and quiet, ready to move forward with no mention of defeat.

Anything less risks reopening wounds that never fully closed.

After that particular strike, I made it a point to reconnect with the departments most affected — not by

walking their halls, but through the eyes and voices of our subject-matter experts who lived it daily.

I listened to their accounts, their exhaustion, their quiet relief.

Sometimes leadership isn't about showing up in person; it's about showing up in presence, being the calm that steadies those who must steady others.

The message was simple: We're still here. Let's rebuild.

Rebuilding after conflict isn't about policies; it's about people.

It's the quiet nods in the cafeteria, the supervisors who model patience, the HR team that answers questions without defensiveness.

In those small moments, respect begins to return — not as a demand, but as a decision.

When both sides choose to lead with composure instead of competition, the strike becomes what it should have been all along: a lesson in resilience.

LRD360° Insight: The measure of leadership isn't how you handle power at the table; it's how you restore balance once the table is cleared.

The Leadership Lesson: Control What You Can, Influence What You Must

When faced with a disrupter, you cannot control their behavior, their tone, or their motives, but you can control your response.

That's where leadership lives.

A true leader doesn't let chaos dictate character.

A true leader balances firmness with fairness, patience with purpose.

A true leader protects people — even the ones who misunderstood them.

Both sides left bruised.

The union had proven its ability to mobilize, but its members had lost weeks of pay.

Management had preserved operations, but morale had taken a hit.

Rebuilding trust was now the real negotiation, one without a table, one that required empathy instead of leverage.

The truth is, there are no real winners in a strike.

There are only survivors, each side nursing wounds and quietly wondering how to rebuild what was lost.

The disrupter eventually moved on, leaving behind a unit more divided than before he arrived.

That's the legacy of disruption: temporary power, permanent scars.

But the organization endured because preparation and principle never wavered.

Respect, even when it wasn't reciprocated, became our compass.

Dignity remained nonnegotiable.

LRD360° Insight: Every strike ends, but its aftershocks live in the spaces where leadership hesitates.

Re-humanizing the Workplace

After any labor unrest, one truth always surfaces: People crave normalcy.

They want to know whether the cafeteria is open, whether paychecks will process on time, whether their manager still trusts them.

Restoring order requires visibility, not grand gestures:

Walk the halls.

Host short check-ins.

Acknowledge fatigue.

Honor both the sacrifice and the survival.

Leadership after conflict is less about direction and more about presence.

It's easy to lead during victory; it's harder to lead through recovery.

The employees are watching for proof that leadership learned something too.

LRD360° Insight: Respect isn't rebuilt through declarations; it's rebuilt through demonstration.

Reflection & Leadership Framework: Internal Debrief

When the dust settled after those long days, I sat in my office long after the building had emptied.

The strike had ended, but the aftershock still hummed through every hallway, in the weary looks, the quiet relief, and the unspoken question lingering on both sides: Was it worth it?

That's the question leadership must face after every labor crisis.

Not Who won? but What did we learn?

This is where the best leadership teams are forged.

They don't rewrite history to hide mistakes; they dissect it to prevent repetition.

They identify when emotion overtook reason, when assumptions replaced evidence, when silence was mistaken for strength.

The true post-bargaining debrief isn't about blame; it's about calibration.

It asks: How do we carry the lessons forward without carrying the bitterness with them?

LRD360° Insight: Every negotiation writes a playbook. The great leaders are the ones who actually read theirs.

Closing Reflection

Every disruption tests not just the structure of the contract, but the character of the leadership behind it.

Sabotage thrives in silence, but accountability restores balance. A strategist's calm, not their outrage, determines whether chaos becomes collapse or correction.

LRD360° Insight: When conflict turns corrosive, leadership becomes the antidote. Not the audience.

CHAPTER 6

The Day After the Vote
The Quiet Before the Next Storm

Where Relief Meets Reality; and Leadership Begins Again

When the last picket sign fades and the crowd's echo finally breaks, what remains is not relief but the need to recalibrate.

The disrupter is gone, but the residue of confrontation lingers in the walls, in the pauses between conversations, in the eyes that look but do not yet trust.

And then comes the vote: a clear signal that endurance is entering its next phase. The negotiation's energy does not simply vanish; it reconfigures, shifting the dynamic within the room.

The environment shifts once more: from confrontation to calculation, from survival to stewardship.

The table is cleared, but leadership's test isn't over.

Because after every storm, there is a stillness that demands something rarer than courage: composure.

The Calm After the Clash

The room is quiet now. Posters have come down, coffee cups are stacked in corners, and the echo of late-night laughter lingers like the memory of thunder.

After weeks, sometimes months, of bargaining, both sides feel the strange silence that follows intensity.

It isn't peace.

It's recovery.

That morning after ratification, workplaces feel heavier.

The adrenaline that powered twelve-hour sessions drains away, leaving exhaustion and fragile relief.

People cross hallways with heads up but eyes cautious, like professionals reentering normalcy after a long campaign.

They wonder: Was it worth it? Did we win? What comes next?

Inside every collective-bargaining campaign lives this moment of suspension.

Negotiators trade in language and leverage, but once the ink dries, what remains are stories: interpretations of who fought hardest, who gave most, and who blinked first.

This is the moment leadership matters most, because perception will shape reality faster than any clause in the contract.

LRD360° Insight: Negotiation doesn't end when the deal is signed; it just changes rooms.

When Strategy Becomes Storytelling

Within twenty-four hours of a tentative agreement, strategy gives way to storytelling.

The campaign of persuasion begins anew — not at the table, but in the narrative.

The union becomes the narrator, with stewards, officers, and chief spokespersons now turning from warriors to messengers who translate dense legal text into language stirring hearts.

They must describe gains, contextualize

compromises, and keep enthusiasm alive without overpromising.

Members will read every word for evidence: of victory, of loss, or of betrayal.

The message must strike a precise balance: confident but not arrogant, factual yet hopeful.

The credibility of leadership rests entirely on tone.

Meanwhile, management faces a different test — silence.

The employer must resist the urge to celebrate, explain, or defend.

Even a congratulatory email to supervisors can be misread as gloating.

A single careless quote in the press, "We held the line on wages", can reignite resentment faster than any clause in the contract.

So, while the union tells its story publicly, management must practice quiet discipline internally.

Each side is now managing optics, and both know that one wrong note can sour the entire score.

LRD360° Insight: Silence can be strategy when your credibility is your currency.

The Emotional Undercurrent

Every agreement carries emotion — the invisible current that steadies or capsizes morale.

For employees, the announcement brings curiosity and judgment.

They scroll through group chats and whisper in break rooms, measuring expectations against results.

For managers, it brings relief laced with unease.

They want things to return to normal — but normal has shifted.

This is the bargaining hangover: the emotional residue that follows prolonged confrontation.

Friendships have strained. Rumors have spread.

Negotiation consumes energy like a storm consumes oxygen, and when it's over, the air feels thin.

Great leaders sense this.

They don't rush to declare victory; they steady the room.

They remind teams that contracts are frameworks, not finish lines.

They organize debriefings, express gratitude, invite feedback, and listen most importantly.

A composed leader becomes the emotional barometer of the organization.

When leadership steadies its tone, people exhale.

LRD360° Insight: The tone you set in steady times determines how your team will respond when pressure rises.

Union Leadership: The Art of Selling the Deal

For the union, ratification is its own campaign — one of persuasion, not protest.

The stewards must now convert the long nights and hard stands into tangible progress.

They gather in break rooms, community centers, and virtual meetings, the places where trust still feels personal.

They answer questions about overtime, health care, and scheduling.

They manage not just the numbers, but the narrative of fairness, especially for those who feel left behind.

The key lies in framing: Even compromise can sound like strategy.

"Did we get everything we asked for? No. Did we move the bar higher for the next round? Absolutely."

Transparency breeds patience. Spin breeds rebellion.

The best spokespersons understand that authenticity outperforms charisma.

They show vulnerability, saying, "I wish we could've gotten more, but I'm proud of what we secured together."

That single sentence can turn doubt into solidarity.

And yes. Small gestures matter. Pizza in the union hall, coffee in the break room.

These aren't tokens; they're rituals of recovery.

Because people remember not only what was said, but how they felt when it was said.

LRD360° Insight: After conflict, people don't need perfection; they need proof of good faith.

Management Leadership: The Discipline of Restraint

For management, the path forward is quieter — but no less strategic.

The message must project unity without arrogance, gratitude without gloating.

Executives should acknowledge the hard work of both sides while reaffirming fiscal prudence and mutual respect.

No victory laps.

No "We contained costs" headlines.

In the public sector, the pressure multiplies.

Leaders must balance three audiences at once: employees, taxpayers, and the governing body that approves the deal.

Each group brings its own expectations and political filters.

One careless comment can undo months of disciplined diplomacy.

The best leaders use empathy as their language of restraint.

They prepare talking points anchored in shared values: responsibility, fairness, and stability.

They brief department heads early, aligning tone before anyone speaks publicly.

They model composure, thanking negotiators, staff, and even union partners for professionalism and perseverance.

Because respect, when modeled publicly, resonates inward.

It reinforces culture more effectively than any policy memo ever could.

LRD360° Insight: Every post-agreement message either strengthens the bridge or shakes it. Choose words like you're choosing materials for the next span.

The Optics Game

The room is calm now, but the air is charged with attention.

Everyone, employees, taxpayers, reporters, even board members, wants to know what just happened and what it means.

The contract may be tentative, but the headlines are permanent.

At this stage, perception is currency, and credibility is the only reserve that matters.

If bargaining was the storm, communication is the atmosphere that follows.

It can either clear the sky or cloud the next horizon.

Strong leaders understand this truth: Every negotiation lives twice, once at the table, and again in the story told about it.

Those who manage that second life with discipline secure both influence and legacy.

LRD360° Insight: Every agreement lives twice: first in fact, then in perception. Leadership decides which one endures.

The Optics of Victory

Both sides crave validation. The union wants its members to see progress; management wants the public to see prudence.

But in the public arena, nuance rarely trends.

Words like compromise or mutual gain don't make headlines — victory and defeat do.

That's why skilled leaders treat post-bargaining optics as a second negotiation: not over clauses, but over narrative.

The goal isn't spin; it's strategy.

You're managing meaning, not manipulating perception.

The union's message should sound passionate but disciplined: "We fought hard — and we delivered."

The employer's message should sound confident but measured: "We reached an agreement that honors employees and protects fiscal integrity."

Neither should step on the other's narrative.

When one side declares total triumph, it implies the other lost — and every future collaboration begins in distrust.

Wise leaders choreograph their words like movement, each aware that tone today becomes trust tomorrow.

LRD360° Insight: After the deal, every word becomes a precedent. Communicate as if you're already negotiating the next round.

The Anatomy of Perception

In the LRD360° framework, perception operates in three dimensions:

1. Content: what you say — the facts, numbers, and terms.

2. Context: how members, boards, and the public interpret those facts.

3. Conduct: how you behave while delivering them.

All three matter, but conduct dominates.

People forget your talking points long before they forget your tone.

A smirk in a press conference, a defensive answer during Q&A, or an untimely social post can erode credibility faster than any fiscal error.

Effective leaders pre-script not just statements but demeanor.

They decide who speaks, who stays silent, and what emotional energy the message should carry.

You can't control interpretation — but you can control the integrity of delivery.

Perception isn't performance; it's alignment.

When words, actions, and intent match, credibility compounds quietly but unmistakably.

LRD360° Insight: Facts inform trust. Tone sustains it.

Dual Accountability: The Public-Sector Tightrope

In private industry, a contract announcement reaches a defined circle: employees, investors, and analysts.

In the public sector, it's a full arena with competing spotlights and no intermission.

Union leaders must sell the deal internally to members while projecting unity externally.

Management must justify the same deal to a governing board, taxpayers, and the press, each with its own politics and priorities.

Every word becomes dual-use.

When an alderman hears "Employees won significant raises," he braces for headlines that read "County caves to union."

When a member hears "Fiscal restraint prevailed," she wonders whether leadership settled too soon.

The Chief Strategist stands between these narratives, translating numbers into fairness and emotion into logic:

"Yes, wages increased, but turnover will decrease. Stability saves money."
"Yes, health care contributions adjusted, but wellness incentives reduce long-term costs."

This is the art of reframing without distortion — aligning economics with empathy.

Both sides depend on it, because credibility is the only currency that survives both chambers: the public square and the internal hall.

LRD360° Insight: Bridges don't hold because both sides agree; they hold because both sides trust the structure.

The Role of Timing

In post-bargaining communication, timing is the silent amplifier of trust.

The first 72 hours after ratification decide whether momentum builds or dissolves.

Move too fast, and it feels performative.

Move too slowly, and control of the story slips away.

Strategic leaders follow a clear rhythm of release:

1. Internal first. Employees and members deserve to hear directly from leadership before reporters do.

2. Partners second. Department heads and internal influencers receive context to reinforce alignment.

3. Public last. Once internal clarity is strong, the external message can follow.

This sequencing preserves trust.

No one should learn about their own future from a news feed.

When communication flows in this order, credibility compounds — and each audience becomes an ally instead of a risk.

LRD360° Insight: Timing is tone. Deliver too early, and you sound defensive; too late, and you sound detached.

Media Management Without Manipulation

In today's climate, every clause becomes content and every quote becomes commentary.

You can't control the volume of chatter — but you can control clarity.

Strong communicators lead with concise, values-driven statements:

"This agreement reflects our commitment to fairness, fiscal health, and continuity of service."

"We're proud of what collaboration achieved for employees and the public alike."

These statements center shared purpose, not personal victory.

They prevent one side from being cast as the villain in a story that belongs to both.

If misinformation surfaces, "Management caved" or "Union sold out", respond once: calmly, and with facts.

Then pivot the discussion back to principle.

Over-defensiveness signals insecurity; composure signals control.

The most trusted leaders understand that transparency doesn't mean oversharing — it means precision.

Every word must reinforce integrity, not impulse.

LRD360° Insight: In the noise of perception, truth must be your anchor and tone your compass.

Reputation Equity

Every negotiation leaves residue: emotional, cultural, and reputational.

How leaders behave after the deal shapes whether anyone will follow them into the next one.

Executives who issue balanced, gracious statements build credibility that compounds.

Union leaders who celebrate wins without vilifying management earn influence that lasts.

Reputation is cumulative. Every round of bargaining writes another line in your leadership résumé.

People will forget clauses and cost tables, but they'll remember how you carried yourself when the cameras were gone.

They'll remember whether you were fair when you didn't have to be, composed when you could've erupted, respectful when it wasn't returned.

That's reputation equity — credibility stored like capital, quietly accruing interest for the next crisis, the next negotiation, the next test of character.

LRD360° Insight: Your last deal is the résumé for your next.

When Optics Collide

Even the best-planned communications can unravel:

- A reporter distorts a quote.

- A board member speaks off-script.

- A viral post twists context into conflict.

The LRD360° response is composure, not combat.

Gather facts. Align internally. Deliver one message. Once.

Overreaction validates the rumor; calm resets the frame.

Transparency, not theatrics, defines credible institutions.

When leadership stays disciplined, even detractors begin to sound temporary.

LRD360° Insight: Don't fight the rumor. Outlast it with truth.

Optics as Long-Term Strategy

Strong leaders don't treat optics as public relations; they treat them as policy.

Every statement sets precedent. Every communication becomes a case study in credibility.

That's why the LRD360° framework recommends an annual audit: a three-question mirror held to your own institution:

1. Do you believe leadership communicates honestly?

2. Do you feel respected in how information is shared?

3. Do you trust that your interests are considered in decisions?

The answers reveal an organization's emotional balance sheet.

Budgets may renew yearly, but reputations renew daily.

LRD360° Insight: Perception isn't the opposite of reality; it's the lens that magnifies it.

The Return to Work: Turning Paper into Presence

The deal is done. The lights are dim.

For a brief moment, the organization exhales — and then holds that breath again.

Because the ink on paper is only the beginning.

Implementation reveals every weakness the storm disguised.

Each clause must now become behavior; each promise must now become proof.

Leaders who translate policy into presence don't hide behind emails.

They walk halls, listen first, and let steadiness replace spectacle.

They know people trust what they experience far more than what they read.

LRD360° Insight: You can't deposit a contract into the trust bank. You build that balance through what happens after.

From Recovery to Readiness

Every storm leaves behind silence.

But in leadership, silence is never still — it's recalibration.

In those weeks after ratification, as the workplace hums back to rhythm, something else begins to stir beneath the routine.

Supervisors return to schedules.

Employees return to tasks.

And leadership returns to watching — not out of suspicion, but awareness.

Because patterns always repeat.

The same personalities that rallied through conflict will soon define the next challenge.

The same fault lines that trembled under pressure are quietly reforming.

What feels like calm is actually prelude.

Great leaders know this moment: the soft hum before the next storm, the quiet test of vigilance, patience, and preparation.

They review lessons, recalibrate teams, and restore discipline before emotion hardens into apathy.

The most dangerous moment isn't when the room is loud; it's when it seems completely calm.

That's when leaders either drift into comfort or double down on awareness.

Because in labor relations, storms don't end; they evolve.

And leadership's real test isn't surviving conflict; it's sensing its return before anyone else does.

LRD360° Insight: The best time to prepare for the next storm is while the sky still looks clear.

Closing Reflection

Leadership after the storm isn't about speeches or celebration; it's about stillness with purpose.

When the noise fades, influence is measured in how calmly you restore rhythm, how quietly you rebuild confidence, and how steadily you prepare for what comes next.

The real strength of a leader isn't proven in the fight. It's preserved in the calm that follows it.

LRD360° Insight: The truest test of leadership isn't weathering the storm. It's teaching others how to stand when the air is still.

CHAPTER 7

The Second Table

Turning Negotiation into Governance

Where Agreement Ends but Accountability Begins

This is where politics pauses and leadership speaks.

The ink may be dry; the work isn't done.

Once the union ratifies, the story moves to another stage, one where politics, policy, and perception meet. In the public sector, every agreement still needs a second audience: the Legislative Board's approval.

And that room has its own rules, its own optics, and its own definition of leadership.

The Empty Table

The table is empty now.

The papers are signed, the voices gone.

What remains is the echo: of words, choices, and tone.

In the public-sector, the real test of a negotiation doesn't end when the deal is struck.

It begins when the board or legislature receives the documents.

Because what's on paper is only half the story. The other half is what people believe is on paper, and that belief can turn an achievement into an ambush if the optics are not managed with precision and grace.

LRD360° Insight: Negotiation may win the deal, but communication wins the room.

The New Audience

For weeks, you've lived inside the world of bargaining tables, proposals, and counteroffers.

Now you face a different arena: a bipartisan board of elected or appointed officials, finance directors, taxpayers, and media.

Each arrives with its own lens:

- Fiscal conservatives scan for overspending.

- Progressives look for fairness and inclusion.

- Executives seek operational continuity.

- Unions ensure promises are honored.

You're no longer defending numbers. You're defending narrative.

LRD360° Insight: You can't control the votes, but you can shape the story.

Two Bottom Lines: Public vs. Private Logic

In business, the bottom line is profit.

In public service, the bottom line is trust: proven through service.

Every dollar given to workers is seen as a dollar taken from taxpayers — from a mother needing childcare, a senior awaiting home health, a road waiting to be paved.

That duality makes public-sector ratification uniquely complex. It isn't just financial; it's philosophical.

LRD360° Insight: Every budget is a moral statement, not just a math problem.

The Leadership Balancing Act

A legislative board is a body of elected or appointed officials tasked with representing the interests of their constituents, overseeing public policy, and making decisions that affect budgets, services, and labor agreements.

When you stand before such a board, you're no longer simply a negotiator — you're a translator.

You must show how the agreement supports service delivery, stabilizes labor relations, and strengthens morale, without appearing politically indulgent.

Say too little, and you seem evasive.

Say too much, and your words become ammunition.

LRD360° Insight: When you speak to both sides, speak to their values, not their vocabulary.

The Day of the Second and Final Vote

The air in the boardroom feels heavier than usual.

Reporters line the walls. Union members fill the seats.

You can feel decades of distrust hanging in the air.

The chair gavels the meeting to order.

Numbers flash. Someone whispers, "What if they don't pass it?"

You smile, but you know that question isn't hypothetical.

Board ratification, like union ratification, is never guaranteed.

Each vote carries political risk, and the only way through is narrative alignment: proving that this agreement serves people.

LRD360° Insight: Facts appeal to reason. Stories move votes.

The Strategy of Consensus

The boardroom was already divided the moment we arrived — not with anger, but with habit.

Republicans, Democrats, Independents, each carrying the expectations of their constituents and interpreting equity differently.

- Papers were shuffled, whispers exchanged, and eyes darted for alignment that didn't exist.

- The challenge wasn't math; it was mindset.

- Everyone wanted stability.

- No one trusted the path to get there.

Leadership had to step forward, not as an advocate for one side, but as a translator for all: bridging priorities, connecting perspectives, and turning competing visions into a shared purpose. One conversation at a time, doubt began to give way to direction.

LRD360° Insight: Negotiation earns the agreement. Diplomacy earns the future.

Behind the Curtain: Preparation Meets Persuasion

Walking into that boardroom chamber unarmed with context would have been like bringing logic to a debate built on perception.

Located in the City Hall/County building, the room itself demanded attention: rows of chairs occupied by elected officials, each with a microphone poised for speech; a raised dais at the front where the presiding executive or committee chair observed every interaction; the board secretary ready to document the proceedings; and guards stationed along the back wall, a silent reminder that order could not be taken for granted.

So, we began early: one-on-one briefings, small group calls, quiet listening sessions. Each board member, regardless of party, needed to see themselves in the story of this agreement. We didn't just present data; we listened.

We asked:

- "What concerns you most about this deal?"
- "How do you think your constituents will view it?"
- "What would fiscal responsibility look like to you in this context?"

By the time the public meeting arrived, half the board already felt included — not convinced, but connected.

LRD360° Insight: Inclusion before persuasion. That's how consensus begins.

Bridging Opposite Philosophies

Public service isn't villains and heroes; it's competing truths.

One side wants accountability; the other, equity. But both want sustainability.

We framed the deal as risk mitigation:

- Predictable costs for conservatives.
- Investment in human capital for progressives.

When the story was told this way, both sides could claim a win, because both sides had been heard.

LRD360° Insight: Consensus isn't compromise; it's architecture.

The Power of Framing

During my early years in labor, I learned a hard truth: if you don't frame the message, someone else will.

When the news cycle begins, you can't control the headline, but you can write the quote they'll use.

That's why we crafted a communication plan that paired data with dignity.

Our message was simple:

> "This agreement strengthens our workforce, safeguards our taxpayers, and sets a new standard for collaboration."

Not once did we use the words raise, concession, or cost increase.

Instead, we talked about retention, stability, and service continuity.

Those words turned skeptics into supporters.

LRD360° Insight: Language doesn't spin the truth. It gives the truth a fighting chance.

Bipartisan Trust: The 2017 Turning Point

In 2017, our county accomplished something it hadn't seen in decades: unanimous, bipartisan approval of multiple union contracts.

Every commissioner, Democrat and Republican, not only voted yes but moved to add their names as cosponsors of the contract resolution.

It wasn't magic.

It was method.

We didn't lead with partisanship; we led with principles:

- Loyalty to fiscal stability.

- Respect for the workforce.

- Dignity for the taxpayers.

By the time the roll call began, party labels no longer mattered.

People didn't vote for me. They voted for trust.

And trust is the one resource that multiplies when shared.

LRD360° Insight: When trust enters the room, politics exits quietly.

Optics: The Art of Quiet Victory

Once the vote passed, there were no press conferences.

No chest-thumping.

We sent a memo thanking the board, the unions, and the staff for "their shared commitment to stability."

That was enough.

Optics in leadership aren't about hiding success; they're about protecting it.

When you gloat, you invite division.

When you thank, you invite partnership.

Our quiet victory earned long-term goodwill: the kind that carries into the next negotiation.

LRD360° Insight: Celebrate publicly, humbly. Let others tell the story.

The Leadership Equation: Stability Over Spotlight

True leadership isn't about claiming the microphone; it's about mastering the echo.

It's about understanding that credibility compounds through consistency.

The goal wasn't to win one vote. It was to create a blueprint for future collaboration — a rhythm of respect that made every subsequent negotiation easier to start and faster to close.

In the years since, I've applied that model to every high-stakes approval: Start with inclusion, lead with transparency, and finish with gratitude.

That's the rhythm of trust.

LRD360° Insight: The loudest victory is the one that never has to be defended.

The Legacy of Bipartisan Leadership

When the cameras are gone and the applause fades, what remains is what truly defines leadership: trust that endures when no one's keeping score.

That's what bipartisan leadership builds: institutional trust.

Not the kind that lives in headlines, but the kind that allows organizations to function smoothly, even when their leaders change.

It's the most underrated achievement in public service: turning former adversaries into reliable partners and setting a tone of steady, principled governance.

LRD360° Insight: The mark of great leadership isn't how loudly it wins, but how quietly it lasts.

The Calm After the Vote

After that 2017 vote, the unanimous, bipartisan approval that defied expectation; the legislative chamber didn't erupt in cheers. It exhaled.

Union representatives hugged quietly in the back of the room.

Commissioners who rarely spoke nodded to each other across the aisle.

Even the reporters hesitated before filing their stories, unsure how to write about agreement instead of conflict.

In that moment, it was clear: The purpose of leadership isn't to prove who's right; it's to create a space where everyone can do what's right.

LRD360° Insight: Agreement is the byproduct of understanding, not its substitute.

From Approval to Accountability

Ratification is only the beginning of implementation.

Once the board signs off, the next test begins: turning language into action and commitments into conduct.

A leader's responsibility doesn't end when the motion passes; it expands.

You must steward what you negotiated, guide your teams through the transition, and keep every party aligned to the spirit of the agreement.

Too often, leaders celebrate the win and walk away.

That's when confusion fills the vacuum, and good faith erodes.

The legacy of bipartisan leadership depends on what happens after the vote:

- Follow through on commitments.
- Keep communication open.
- Maintain fairness in implementation.

Those post-vote choices determine whether credibility compounds or collapses.

LRD360° Insight: Winning the vote is a milestone; keeping the trust is the mission.

Political Courage vs. Political Theater

True courage in leadership isn't dramatic.

It's disciplined.

It's the quiet decision to defend balance when one side demands purity.

It's the moment you choose facts over fear and service over self.

In a climate where grandstanding outshines governance, this kind of courage is rare, and it's what sustains institutions through transitions, crises, and even administrations.

Political theater changes headlines.

Political courage changes outcomes.

LRD360° Insight: Leaders who chase applause lose altitude; those who chase alignment gain legacy.

When Leadership Transcends Politics

Every now and then, I'll see a commissioner from that 2017 board.

We've disagreed passionately on later issues, but mutual respect remains anchored in that shared experience.

We proved it was possible to negotiate fairly, honor labor, protect fiscal responsibility, and still leave the table intact.

That memory lingers — not as nostalgia, but as a standard.

Leadership is cyclical.

The players change; the principles shouldn't.

LRD360° Insight: Politics is temporary. Integrity is tenured.

The Quiet Ripple Effect

You can always tell when leadership culture has shifted.

The next time around, negotiations start with less hostility.

Departments collaborate more readily.

The board asks sharper questions but listens longer before judging.

That's the ripple of trust.

You might not see it in real time, but you'll feel it, in the rhythm of meetings, in the tone of disagreement.

When dissent begins to sound like dialogue, that's the signal that something real changed.

LRD360° Insight: The true test of leadership is what people do when you're not in the room.

The 360° Perspective

When dealing with elected bipartisan leadership, it isn't about standing in the middle; it's about standing tall enough to see both sides clearly.

That's what the LRD360° Strategy demands:

- Loyalty to the institution and its mission.
- Respect for every stakeholder's voice.
- Dignity for the people whose lives depend on your decisions.

The 360° lens means you don't just negotiate policy; you manage emotion, perception, and consequence.

It's leadership that looks around corners and still keeps everyone moving forward.

That perspective turns transactional governance into transformational leadership.

LRD360° Insight: A 360° leader doesn't avoid sides; they align them.

Sustaining Trust Across Seasons

Leadership longevity isn't measured in years served; it's measured in stability sustained.

A great leader prepares their organization to thrive long after they're gone.

That means institutionalizing trust, teaching the next generation to lead with the same balance, fairness, and clarity.

You don't just teach how to negotiate; you teach why it matters.

You model that politics may shift, but professionalism must remain constant.

You make dignity the throughline between administrations.

That's when the LRD360° Strategy stops being a framework and becomes a culture.

LRD360° Insight: Legacy leadership is when your successors don't need your presence to follow your principles.

A Note on Humility

Humility is the last and hardest trait to master.

It's easy to preach it from the podium; harder to live it after a major win.

But humility keeps leaders from becoming the story.

It keeps the focus on the mission, the employees, the people.

After the 2017 vote, there was no victory lap, just the quiet work of implementation.

Because the moment you make it about you, you lose the power to make it about everyone else.

LRD360° Insight: Humility isn't weakness; it's wisdom in its quietest form.

Closing Reflection

Looking back, those bipartisan victories weren't just milestones, they reflected what leadership can look like when guided by Loyalty, Respect, and Dignity.

These principles don't belong to any party or profession. They belong to anyone willing to lead with courage, consistency, and care.

The lesson is simple but eternal:

When you lead with integrity, the table holds.

When you lead with empathy and dignity, the room listens and the legacy lasts.

LRD360° Insight: Lead so well that the next leader's job is easier, not harder.

From Governance to Legacy

The applause has faded.

The boardroom lights dim. A new day begins like any other. Yet something subtle has shifted.

The institution operates with steadier rhythm, decisions move more smoothly, and quiet confidence replaces old suspicion.

That's the power of principled governance: when trust becomes infrastructure.

Leadership isn't remembered by how it argued, but by what it sustained.

And as one cycle ends, another always begins — testing whether the lessons learned in victory can survive the silence that follows.

LRD360° Insight: Governance is the echo of negotiation, the lasting sound of how leaders chose to lead when the microphones were turned off.

CHAPTER 8

The Courage to Communicate
The Silence After the Storm

Where Silence Becomes Story; Unless Leaders Speak First

When the ink finally dries and the signatures fade into the archive, the next test of leadership begins, not at the table, but in the echo that follows it.

Because every agreement, new or renewed, lives or dies by how it's communicated.

The same courage that brought leaders back to the table must now guide them back to their people.

If negotiation tested discipline, what follows will test connection.

This is where negotiation becomes narrative, and where silence, if left unattended, can undo everything leadership just restored.

LRD360° Insight: The hardest part of leadership isn't reaching agreement; it's keeping people aligned after you do.

The Silence After the Storm

The storm has passed. The contract is signed. The cameras have stopped flashing.

And yet something still **hums** beneath the quiet: uncertainty. Every organization feels it.

The quiet that follows major change isn't peace; it's processing. Employees retreat to corners; supervisors interpret new directives in half-truths; and managers begin rewriting narratives in hallway whispers.

LRD360° Insight: Silence after conflict isn't calm; it's compression.

Leadership in this phase requires courage: the courage to speak when the room wants quiet, and to listen when the room finally starts to murmur again.

The Leadership Vacuum

Immediately after a major negotiation, leaders often make a dangerous assumption: People already know.

They don't.

Teams may have been copied on every email, sat in every meeting, even heard the ratification speech. But comprehension lags behind information. Employees are still translating policy into impact:

- "What does this mean for my schedule?"

- "Does this change my pay?"

- "Will my manager treat me differently now?"

When leadership fails to fill that vacuum with clarity, speculation rushes in. That's how misinformation metastasizes. HR professionals call it the post-bargaining lag. I call it the fog: the moment when people start writing their own endings to a story that leadership hasn't finished telling.

LRD360° Insight: If you don't tell the story, someone else will; and they won't be kind to your plot.

The Cost of Quiet

Silence has a cost, and it's measurable.

Productivity drops. Morale dips. Supervisors spend hours clarifying rumors instead of leading teams. A five-minute clarification could save a week of confusion.

Consider a large urban hospital system after a contentious bargaining cycle. Once the agreement was ratified, leadership went silent: no memos, no town halls, no follow-up. Within weeks, the rumor mill filled the gap:

- "Management coming to our homes for home checks when we call off"

- "We lost our shift differentials."

- "We are losing our comp time"

- "The union gave up too much."

None of it was true. But perception became reality, and grievances spiked astronomically within a month. By the time leadership reengaged, trust had eroded. It wasn't policy failure; it was communication failure.

The Courage to Step into Discomfort

In the aftermath of conflict, communication feels risky. Emotions are raw; words can reopen wounds.

That's why so many leaders retreat. They mistake quiet for recovery.

The opposite is true.

The longer leaders wait to reengage, the harder it becomes to reconnect.

Courage in leadership isn't just about holding the line at the bargaining table; it's about facing the human aftermath.

It means showing up at roll calls, staff meetings, and break rooms. It means standing before people who may still be angry and choosing transparency over comfort.

LRD360° Insight: The strongest leaders don't avoid the echo; they answer it.

From Transaction to Translation

A collective bargaining agreement or policy decision is a transaction.

But explaining it — that's translation.

Leadership must become fluent in simplifying complexity.

Instead of "the wage-adjustment formula," say, "You'll see the increase in your second check of the month."

Instead of "modified step progression," say, "Your anniversary date now triggers advancement automatically."

Employees don't want management to sound smart; they want management to sound clear. Communication that humanizes complexity builds confidence faster than any press release ever could.

LRD360° Insight: Complexity may impress, but clarity connects.

The Role of Tone

Tone is leadership's most underestimated tool. When people are tense, they don't listen for words; they listen for tone.

An anxious leader spreads panic.

A defensive leader invites defiance.

A calm leader signals stability.

Tone sets the emotional thermostat of the workplace. After high-stakes negotiations, that thermostat runs hot. The leader's job is to cool it, not by minimizing the heat, but by managing it.

Every meeting, memo, and message is a cue. Employees read between every line:

- "Do they sound confident?"
- "Do they sound resentful?"
- "Do they sound like they still care?"

LRD360° Insight: Your tone is your tell.

The Power of Listening Tours

Reengagement begins with listening. A listening tour isn't corporate jargon; it's repair work.

Gather small groups where people can speak candidly. No PowerPoints. No scripts. Just space.

Ask questions like:

- "What part of the agreement surprised you?"

- "What's unclear about the rollout?"

- "What can leadership do differently next time?"

The act of asking does two things: it disarms cynicism and uncovers buried truth.

Most employees don't expect their feedback to change policy, but they do expect it to be heard.

Listening converts hostility into dialogue. It transforms us vs. them into we'll figure it out together.

LRD360° Insight: You can't manage what people won't tell you; and they won't tell you if they don't trust you.

The Reemergence of Informal Leaders

Every workplace has two structures: the chart on paper, and the network that actually runs things.

After negotiations, pay attention to the second one: the informal leaders who shape opinions in break rooms, chat threads, and shift changes.

These are your culture carriers.

If they buy in, the message travels. If they don't, the message fractures.

Smart leaders bring them in early. They brief them privately, preview communications, ask for their input. It honors their influence and ensures the message spreads organically.

LRD360° Insight: If you don't recruit your influencers, they'll recruit against you.

Transparency as Strategy

Transparency is not weakness; it's architecture.

It builds structure around uncertainty and signals that leadership has nothing to hide and everything to share.

This doesn't mean oversharing. It means answering questions that already exist before they metastasize into suspicion.

Say: "Here's what we know, here's what we're still figuring out, and here's when you'll hear from us again."

That simple formula converts anxiety into trust.

LRD360° Insight: Clarity calms.

Leading the Message

When the noise subsides, a subtler challenge begins: defining what the storm meant.

Every negotiation, crisis, or major policy shift creates competing versions of truth.

One is written in the contract; the others live in perception.

Leaders who master this phase understand that communication isn't about words; it's about meaning.

LRD360° Insight: Silence invites stories. Strategy writes them.

Owning the Narrative

After any major decision, three stories emerge:

1. The official one: the memo or press release.

2. The informal one: the break room version.

3. The public one: the headline or tweet.

The goal isn't to erase the other two: it's to align them through honesty and consistency.

Avoid spin. People sense when they're being sold a version of the truth instead of the truth itself.

Real language beats rehearsed talking points.

When a CEO says, "We listened and we learned," and then details what was learned, credibility grows.

When they say, "We moved forward with mutual respect" without evidence, the message floats.

LRD360° Insight: Every leader has two voices: the one that talks and the one people believe.

Media Management vs. Message Leadership

Media relations isn't about controlling reporters. It's about controlling your own house first.

Because once the press calls, they're not really asking about the deal, but testing your alignment.

In the public sector, statements often pass through layers: communications, legal, and political teams. By the time they reach the public, they sound like a committee that forgot the audience was human.

Strong leaders reverse the process: They write the core message themselves, then let others refine it.

Because voice can't be outsourced.

LRD360° Insight: You can delegate writing but never tone.

Internal Alignment Before External Broadcast

Before you talk to the press, talk to your people.

When employees hear news about their own organization from the media, trust evaporates.

No matter how polished the external message, internal silence makes it hollow.

A Chief Strategist ensures the internal memo drops before the press release.

Town halls should follow within twenty-four hours. Questions should be welcomed, not deflected.

The sequence matters: Union → Employees → Board → Public.

That order isn't political; it's psychological. It tells people closest to the work they come first.

LRD360° Insight: Respect begins with who you tell first.

Message Discipline in a Fragmented World

In the age of screenshots and leaks, one careless sentence can reshape an entire bargaining cycle.

Leaders need message discipline, not censorship but clarity.

Message discipline means everyone on your leadership team can answer three questions without contradiction:

1. What did we agree to?

2. Why did we agree to it?

3. How does it help our people and our mission?

If your directors, supervisors, and union partners can answer those consistently, you control the narrative.

If they can't, the story controls you.

LRD360° Insight: Clarity travels faster than rumors.

When Transparency and Tact Collide

Not every truth belongs in a press release.

Sometimes you owe the public transparency and your employees context.

That's the space where leadership lives.

A public statement should never embarrass your partners or your people. It should protect relationships while telling the truth.

The goal is to explain without exposing, to share enough to build confidence, not enough to damage trust.

This balance matters most in public bargaining. The taxpayer deserves clarity on spending, but employees deserve dignity in how that story is told.

Example: Press Release Framing

✖ Ineffective (Transparency without Tact)

"The County reached an agreement with the nurses' union following months of tension. The new contract reins in costly overtime and establishes tighter attendance rules to reduce budget waste."

This version is technically factual, but the tone is punitive. It implies blame, reinforces division, and erodes goodwill just as collaboration is needed most.

☑ Effective (Transparency with Tact)

"The County and the nurses' union have reached a responsible agreement that balances fiscal accountability with quality patient care. The contract invests in staffing stability, supports employee wellness, and strengthens our shared commitment to serving the community."

This version still conveys fiscal responsibility but frames it as shared stewardship — preserving trust while affirming both public and workforce values.

LRD360° Insight: Transparency without tact is just a press conference.

Bridging Politics and Purpose

Every public institution lives between two loyalties: mission and politics.

A bipartisan board demands language that transcends party lines.

Fiscal conservatives listen for responsibility; labor advocates listen for fairness.

The LRD360° leader speaks to both without betraying either.

Years earlier, during one of the most divided boards I'd served, we found language that transcended party lines. We framed fiscal responsibility and fairness as shared values, not rival agendas.

We framed wage increases as investments in stability, not spending.

We connected benefit changes to retention and continuity of service.

Each phrase honored the values of both sides without distorting the truth.

That isn't political maneuvering. It's message leadership.

LRD360° Insight: If you speak the language of values, everyone understands you.

The Art of Reframing

Language can shift entire perspectives.

Instead of "cost of living adjustment," say "inflation protection."

Instead of "concessions," say "collaborative savings."

Instead of "discipline," say "standards of excellence."

These aren't euphemisms: they're translations of meaning.

Reframing doesn't change facts; it clarifies intent.

When leaders reframe effectively, they don't protect image: they protect impact.

LRD360° Insight: Reframing isn't spin. It's stewardship of meaning.

Social Media: The New Front Line

A post travels faster than any press conference, and its ripple can reshape perception before facts catch up.

The modern leader understands that social media isn't an afterthought; it's a stage.

Use it to humanize, not sanitize. Show your presence in real spaces: visiting departments, thanking staff, explaining decisions in plain language.

If people see you as accessible, they won't believe the echo chamber. Hide behind press releases, and you become

the headline instead of the source.

LRD360° Insight: Visibility is the new credibility.

When Everything Goes Wrong

Even the best message can derail under pressure.

A supervisor misspeaks. A blogger misquotes. A post goes viral for the wrong reason.

Don't panic. Don't lash out. Correct with grace and facts.

The public forgives mistakes faster than evasions.

Employees trust leaders who stand by their words under fire more than those who hide behind consultants.

LRD360° Insight: Integrity is the only message that can't be misquoted.

Communication as Culture

When the headlines fade and the memos are archived, what remains is culture: the invisible current that carries an organization forward or drags it back.

If leadership in crisis is about clarity, leadership in calm is about consistency.

Communication isn't an event. It's oxygen. When leaders withhold it, trust suffocates.

LRD360° Insight: Culture isn't built by what you announce; it's built by what you repeat.

Beyond Crisis Mode

Most organizations communicate only when they must: after a negotiation, during a scandal, and before an audit.

But leadership that waits for crisis is already behind.

Courageous communication means speaking before the fire starts. It means predictable updates, visible leadership, and dialogue that feels routine, not reactive. Think of it as an organizational "tweet schedule": messages land on a steady cadence, so employees don't brace for impact every time a memo drops.

Clarity becomes the norm, not the exception.

LRD360° Insight: You don't earn trust with the message; you earn it with the rhythm.

Building the Feedback Loop

Every leader says they value feedback. Few systematize it.

The strongest organizations treat feedback like a supply chain; it must move in both directions or the system collapses.

After each major initiative, create three checkpoints:

1. Frontline Pulse: Frontline supervisors conduct quick conversations or micro-surveys with those closest to the work.

2. Supervisor Sync: Mid-level leaders gather recurring issues and patterns.

3. Executive Reflection: Senior leaders review trends, not anecdotes, and decide what needs adjustment.

When employees see their input shape action, they don't just feel heard — they feel respected.

LRD360° Insight: Feedback unacknowledged becomes resentment.

The Manager's Mouthpiece Problem

Managers translate leadership intent. If they don't understand the why, they'll rewrite it in the how.

Hold leadership briefings before information cascades downward.

Let managers ask hard questions and shape the language themselves.

Authenticity travels farther than memorized talking points.

LRD360° Insight: Managers don't echo messages; they embody them.

Storytelling as Leadership Practice

Facts inform; stories inspire. Data tells what happened. Stories tell why it matters.

When leaders tie every update to a human outcome — a patient helped, a public service improved, a family supported — communication becomes purpose, not policy.

Storytelling isn't sentimentality. It's strategy.

LRD360° Insight: Every memo should point back to mission.

Transparency in Transition

When organizations restructure or evolve, anxiety fills the silence faster than information.

Leaders often delay updates until every answer is known, but by then, rumors have already multiplied. "They're going to lay us off." "Management's hiding something."

Courageous communication during transition means saying:

"We don't have every detail yet, but here's what we do know and here's when you'll know more."

That single sentence stops fear from metastasizing.

LRD360° Insight: People can handle bad news. They can't handle no news.

The Listening Economy

In the new workplace, attention is currency. Employees invest where they feel seen.

If leaders only broadcast and never respond, they're not communicating — they're advertising.

The LRD360° approach reframes leadership as a listening economy: The more you invest in hearing, the more you earn in influence.

Listening isn't passive. It's the most assertive act of leadership because it invites accountability.

When leaders summarize what they've heard, "Here's what we learned, here's what we're changing," they demonstrate humility and control in equal measure.

LRD360° Insight: Listening doesn't slow you down; it keeps you from circling back.

Embedding Communication in Daily Rituals

Culture is what you do without thinking. To embed communication, make it habitual:

- Weekly Updates: short, predictable notes from leadership.

- Open-Door Fridays: scheduled time for unscripted questions.

- Recognition Moments: celebrations of small wins in real time.

- Union–Management Coffee Talks: informal joint updates that normalize collaboration.

These rituals require intention, not budget. Over time, they shift an organization from reactive to relational.

LRD360° Insight: Culture is just communication repeated long enough to feel like tradition.

Repairing When Communication Fails

Even the best communicators stumble. An email misses empathy. A leak beats the official memo.

The test isn't perfection; it's response. Acknowledge quickly. Clarify factually. Reengage personally.

A simple statement like, "We missed the mark in how we shared that news; here's what we should have said," restores more credibility than any polished correction ever will.

LRD360° Insight: When you own your mistakes, your people will own your mission.

Communication as Leadership Legacy

Every great organization eventually forgets who negotiated which deal, but it never forgets how leadership made people feel afterward.

Communication is the bridge between technical success and emotional memory.

It's what turns management into mentorship, and policy into culture.

Leaders who master it leave behind more than a contract. They leave behind trust.

LRD360° Insight: The true mark of leadership is how the story is told when you're no longer in the room.

Closing Reflection: From Clarity to Connection

Courageous communication doesn't end when the message is sent; it begins when people start living it.

The true test of leadership isn't the meeting at the table. It's the quiet that follows when employees interpret silence as a signal.

When communication becomes rhythm, not reaction, it turns policy into practice.

That's when trust becomes measurable, not in memos, but in behavior.

LRD360° Insight: The contract sets the structure. The conversation keeps it alive.

Great leaders understand that every message is a rehearsal for the next moment of pressure.

They don't communicate to conclude; they communicate to connect.

Because leadership isn't the echo after the storm; it's the steadiness that keeps people believing when calm feels uncertain.

CHAPTER 9

Leadership on the Clock
Don't Let Contracts Expire

Where Time Tests Leadership More Than Any Proposal Ever Could

The Illusion of Stability

Leadership is often tested not by the storms that hit but by the calm that convinces you they won't.

Few situations appear as harmless as operating under an expired collective bargaining agreement. It feels deceptively peaceful. Everyone still reports to work. Paychecks clear. Supervisors give direction. Routine becomes a lullaby. But silence isn't stability; it's suspended motion.

LRD360° Insight: Silence after a contract expires isn't peace. It's the sound of trust thinning.

The Comfort Trap

When a collective bargaining agreement expires, no one should exhale, but many do.

The absence of active bargaining feels deceptively calm, yet expiration marks the most precarious stage of labor peace. At that moment, either party can issue notice to terminate the agreement, triggering the right to strike or lockout. What looks like quiet is really the tightening of risk.

Leaders who mistake delay for safety invite volatility. "Operating under the status quo" sounds stable, but it's a legal fiction: an arrangement held together by mutual restraint, not mutual confidence. Every day that passes without movement increases exposure and uncertainty. The longer the silence, the louder the consequences become.

The Dangers in Delay

Delays erode stability.

Operating under an expired contract buys time but sells out stability. Every unresolved clause becomes a quiet liability.

In the private sector, it may erupt as a strike; in the public sector, it seeps into budgets and policies until confidence erodes. The longer the pause, the louder the uncertainty.

Deferred costs don't disappear. Step increases, cost-of-living adjustments, and retroactive pay don't vanish; they accumulate, quietly compounding until they crash into the balance sheet. What looks like short-term savings soon becomes tomorrow's deficit. Delay doesn't reduce the cost; it redistributes it to the future.

Avoidance undermines credibility. Both union and management think they're avoiding risk. In reality, they're signaling hesitation. Employees sense it; taxpayers read it. When leaders appear afraid to bargain, confidence drops in both directions. Avoidance doesn't preserve credibility; it erodes it.

LRD360° Insight: Status Quo isn't stability. It's suspended risk.

When Silence Replaces Leadership

A lapsed contract exposes character more than conditions. It shows who leads through discomfort and who hides in it.

Great leaders treat expiration as ignition, not retreat. They know silence is more dangerous than disagreement because silence spreads into rumor, resentment, and resistance. By the time it's visible, it's expensive.

LRD360° Insight: Leadership doesn't expire when the contract does.

Dual Lenses: Management and Labor

Expired contracts mirror complacency more than conflict. Both sides convince themselves of the same lie: "It's safer to wait." But safety is rarely found in stillness.

LRD360° Insight: When both sides mistake stillness for safety, leadership becomes the only thing that can move them.

The Employer's Perspective: Budgets and Optics

When a contract lapses, management's instinct is fiscal.

Leaders face spreadsheets, forecasts, and political scrutiny that make every dollar feel like a test of discipline. Delay masquerades as prudence: "Let's wait for next quarter," "We can't open all contracts at once." Each phrase sounds strategic but signals hesitation.

The Budget Mirage

Forecasts built on expired terms are guesswork.

Raises, benefits, and step progressions float in limbo. Finance teams "plug in assumptions," but assumptions aren't agreements, and uncertainty doesn't stay contained to spreadsheets.

Auditors start asking questions. Rating agencies take note. What begins as a temporary hold on negotiations can ripple into the organization's credibility with lenders and investors.

Even a hint of instability can affect bond ratings and borrowing costs, turning delay into a fiscal liability.

LRD360° Insight: Postponed bargaining is deferred maintenance: cheaper today, costlier tomorrow.

The Optics Trap

From the outside, an expired contract looks like failure.

To avoid headlines, leadership goes silent. But silence in a unionized workplace is never neutral; it reads as fear or indifference.

When employers say nothing, others fill the void, and usually louder.

LRD360° Insight: If you don't narrate the silence, someone else will.

The Union's Perspective: Pressure and Perception

For unions, expiration carries a different weight: emotional, not fiscal. Members measure leadership in results, not process.

Every month under status quo feels like a loss. When wages stagnate while rent, gas, and groceries climb, the quiet starts to sound like betrayal. Pressure flows upward: from members to stewards, stewards to union business agents, business agents to elected representatives and the union president, and finally to the chief spokesperson.

The Credibility Clock

Time under an expired contract doesn't just tick; it erodes. Leaders are forced to answer the same question in every meeting: "When will bargaining resume?"

The explanations may be valid (budget cycles, leadership transitions, arbitration delays) but nuance doesn't matter. What members feel is neglect.

Once trust drops, militancy rises. A simple update meeting becomes a referendum on leadership.

LRD360° Insight: When members lose faith in their leaders, they don't go quiet; they go elsewhere for power.

The Pressure to Prove Strength

To reassert credibility, unions often turn to visibility: one-day strikes, pickets, press statements.

The goal is twofold: remind management of unity and reassure members that leadership is fighting. These tactics reenergize but also polarize.

When the contract finally returns to the table, it's no longer about clauses; it's about redemption.

LRD360° Insight: Every month you wait to bargain, tone compounds like interest; and the first payment is always trust.

From Stalemate to Strategy

When both sides delay, a quiet stalemate forms. Supervisors start interpreting gray areas; employees test limits; HR becomes referee.

Slowly, the workplace evolves beyond the contract itself. Neither side controls it anymore.

Negotiations become defensive, not visionary. You're not building the future; you're patching the present.

LRD360° Insight: When leadership delays structure, culture fills the vacuum.

Reclaiming Momentum

Recovery begins with decisive transparency:

1. Set a timeline and announce it. Even if bargaining isn't ready to start, commit publicly to a date. Silence breeds speculation; timelines breed accountability.

2. Reengage informally. Not all dialogue requires the formal table. Side meetings or joint task forces rebuild trust quietly.

3. Acknowledge the lapse. Pretending nothing happened deepens resentment. Simple honesty, "We know this contract expired, and we're fixing it," restores credibility.

4. Reframe the restart. Don't call it starting over. Call it finishing what we began.

LRD360° Insight: Leaders don't reset, they reengage.

Maturity in Motion

Every expired contract tells a story, not of money, but of maturity. It's where leadership stops being procedural and becomes personal.

Great leaders recognize that renewal is not about recovery; it's about evolution.

LRD360° Insight: Leadership maturity begins when patience replaces panic and purpose replaces pride.

The Courage to Restart

The first step back to the table always feels heavier than the last one that ended it. It requires courage to reopen old wounds and admit that delay served no one.

Managers wait for permission. Leaders create momentum. Saying "It's time to fix this" isn't weakness; it's clarity.

The room doesn't need perfection; it needs truth.

LRD360° Insight: The most powerful words a leader can say are, "I see it, and we will fix it."

Trust After Delay

Trust doesn't require speeches; it requires micro-moments, showing up prepared, communicating clearly, and keeping small commitments.

Alignment becomes apology; consistency becomes proof.

When reliability repeats itself, trust returns.

LRD360° Insight: Predictability is the new apology.

Resetting the Narrative

The story of renewal must begin with balance, not blame.

Instead of saying, "We've been under an expired agreement for eighteen months," say, "We're entering this new phase with what we've learned from the last eighteen months."

That shift reframes regret as readiness, and readiness inspires confidence.

LRD360° Insight: Leaders rewrite history by choosing how they tell it.

From Expiration to Evolution

An expired contract can become an accelerant for innovation.

Smart leaders use the gap to modernize language, reimagine processes, and realign purpose.

They ask:

- What language no longer fits our workforce?
- Which provisions were born from old fears, not current realities?
- Where can we build flexibility instead of rigidity?

Instead of "renewing" the past, they design what's next.

Some organizations even use the lapse to introduce hybrid-work clauses, flexible scheduling, or joint labor-management committees.

The gap becomes a bridge, not a scar.

LRD360° Insight: Expiration doesn't end a contract. It invites a redesign.

The Emotional Equation

When contracts lapse, issues stop being procedural and become personal.

A grievance about hours becomes about being

unseen. A complaint about overtime becomes about respect.

Emotion is data, and leaders who recognize it early regain logic faster. Acknowledging how people feel is not surrender; it's strategy.

LRD360° Insight: Acknowledging emotion isn't losing control; it's regaining it.

The Discipline of Documentation

When time passes without agreement, institutional memory fades. Retirements, transfers, and turnover leave behind assumptions instead of clarity.

That's why disciplined documentation becomes leadership insurance.

Track interim understandings, exceptions, and informal practices.

Codify what was improvised. It prevents arguments later and saves thousands in arbitration.

LRD360° Insight: If it isn't written, it's waiting to be misunderstood.

The Culture Cost of Complacency

Working under expired terms breeds quiet decay. Supervisors improvise rules; employees test limits.

Soon, every policy becomes "negotiable", not by design but by neglect.

When structure softens, cynicism hardens.

Leadership must treat expiration as an alert, not for panic, but for prevention.

LRD360° Insight: When structure is optional, respect becomes negotiable.

Turning Expiration into Evolution

To recover, leadership must embrace three disciplines:

1. Transparency before Trust: Share the why behind delays and the how behind next steps.

2. Empathy before Efficiency: People won't follow until they feel heard. Listen first.

3. Action before Applause: Move decisively; clarity will follow.

These habits transform lapse into renewal. They rebuild accountability and turn organizational fatigue into focus.

LRD360° Insight: Recovery is leadership's greatest performance review.

The LRD360° Test of Maturity

When contracts expire, the true test begins:

- Loyalty: to mission, not comfort.

- Respect: for dissenting voices, not just agreeable ones.

- Dignity: in tone and treatment, even when frustration peaks.

These principles convert breakdown into breakthrough. Dignity, once demonstrated, becomes contagious.

LRD360° Insight: Mature leaders aren't calm because they lack emotion; they're calm because they've mastered meaning.

Closing Reflection: From Expiration to Excellence

Contracts expire. Markets shift. People move on. But leadership endures when it's practiced, not just preached.

The true cost of an expired agreement isn't financial; it's relational.

And the cure isn't money; it's maturity.

When leaders use expiration as an opportunity to show courage, accountability, and empathy, the organization emerges stronger than before.

Because in the end, every contract is temporary; but culture is forever.

LRD360° Insight: A leader's legacy isn't measured by how long the contract lasted, but by how well the trust did.

CHAPTER 10

Beyond the Table
What Leadership Leaves Behind

Where Culture Outlives Contracts; and Legacy Takes Shape

Every table tells a story: of courage, calculation, and compromise.

But the real measure of leadership begins after the gavel falls.

When the room empties and the applause fades, what remains is culture, the invisible residue of how people were treated when the stakes were highest.

LRD360° Insight: Leadership doesn't end at agreement; it begins in the aftermath.

As discussed in previous chapters, the most successful leaders understand that bargaining is only a rehearsal for everything that follows.

The same habits that kept tempers steady at the table now shape the foundation of leadership: clarity, empathy, and tone.

If communication fails, all that strategy collapses into noise.

If dignity disappears, every clause you fought for loses its meaning.

LRD360° Insight: Clarity keeps systems running; dignity keeps people believing.

After a hard-won contract or crisis resolution, organizations crave consistency.

Teams watch to see whether the promises made under pressure, will still hold in calm.

That is the true "implementation phase": not of policy, but of trust.

As we saw in earlier chapters, the leader's job isn't finished when the ink dries; it simply changes form.

Leaders who narrate change openly, who explain decisions in plain language, convert uncertainty into alignment.

LRD360° Insight: The same words that built agreement must now build understanding.

Beyond the table, leadership becomes translation.

You translate vision into practice, direction into rhythm, and policy into purpose.

What was negotiated in hours must now be lived for years.

That's why every leader needs a post-table discipline: to keep communication predictable, gratitude visible, and accountability mutual.

LRD360° Insight: Leadership maturity is measured in follow-through.

The lessons endure across every field:

- Preparation builds credibility.

- Transparency sustains morale.

- Respect preserves momentum.

These are not bargaining tactics; they are life systems.

They turn one-time victories into durable cultures.

And they travel from the break room to the boardroom, from public service to professional sports, wherever human stakes meet organizational pressure.

LRD360° Insight: The methods change; the mindset endures.

The next chapter doesn't shift away from these lessons; it brings them to life.

Because whether you're negotiating a public-sector contract or an NFL deal, the principles remain the same: Loyalty, Respect, and Dignity.

LRD360° Insight: What you practice in the quiet rooms decides how you perform under the bright lights.

Closing Reflection

Every leader leaves fingerprints on the culture they build: not in signatures or speeches, but in how people feel when the pressure lifts.

The real legacy of negotiation isn't written in contracts; it's written in conduct. Because long after the table is cleared, people remember how they were led, not what they were told.

LRD360° Insight: Deals end. Dignity endures.

CHAPTER 11

Negotiating with Zeros on the Line
Lessons from the Field

Where High Stakes Reveal the Leader; Not the Title

The Field of Leadership

Every negotiation has a stage. For years mine was the conference room: white walls, a ticking clock, and the accumulated tension of many in a room, each person carrying their own version of fairness.

But the moment I stepped into a National Football League facility not as a fan but as a certified contract advisor (the person certified by the NFL Players Association to negotiate players' contracts) I felt it immediately. The air carried the weight of adrenaline and ambition. The stakes were louder. The zeros were real not just in budgets, but on the backs of jerseys.

In that moment, I didn't see a game; I saw individuals: each man carrying his own story, his own stakes, his own version of victory. My role shifted from spectator to shield. I was no longer rooting for a team; I was standing guard for the player, invested not in the scoreboard but in the human being behind the helmet.

This wasn't collective bargaining in the hospital or courthouse. This was combat in suits. A rookie's deal could set the tone for his career. An assistant coach's clause could define whether his family stayed or moved. Every decision came with six or seven zeros attached, yet the same human dynamics from every labor table still applied: fear, trust, and the constant struggle for respect.

LRD360° Insight: Whether it's a hospital or a huddle, leadership begins when power meets pressure.

From the Break Room to the Locker Room

Public-sector bargaining and professional sports negotiations are not as far apart as they appear.

In both, you're negotiating human potential. In one world, you fight over contract language about "mandatory overtime." In the other, you fight over "off-season conditioning requirements."

The stakes differ but the principles are identical: stability, fairness, and longevity. Both sides want to win; the smart ones aim to sustain. In the NFL, I quickly learned that winning a deal too aggressively, squeezing every drop out of the other side, could destroy future opportunities. You have to negotiate like you'll see that GM again ... because you will.

LRD360° Insight: You can't build relationships if you're always spiking the ball.

The Power of Preparation

Before every contract call, preparation was treated like game film.

Every clause, every comma mattered. Player data (rushing yards, receptions, snaps played) revealed leverage, not just history.

In the NFL, incentives are classified as "most likely to be earned" or "least likely to be earned" based on past performance. I studied the club like an opponent: Was it cash-rich but salary-cap-tight? What position did the data reveal as a true need, not just a headline? And I profiled the general manager's tendencies: did he front-load guarantees or bury rewards deep in conditional triggers?

That kind of preparation could mean the difference between a $50,000 signing bonus and a $500,000 one.

In sports, as in government, you must understand personalities as deeply as the policies. The quietest person in the room may hold the most influence. The one cracking jokes may be masking uncertainty.

A great negotiator reads the room and knows when to stop talking.

LRD360° Insight: Silence is often the loudest form of leverage.

Lessons from the League

Negotiating in sports taught me more about leadership than any seminar or boardroom ever could.

In that world, emotion and logic collide in real time. You learn how to manage adrenaline, not eliminate it. You learn that strategy isn't about domination; it's about direction. And you learn that reputation, once lost, takes longer to rebuild than any player's ACL.

That's why the discipline from public-sector negotiations never left; it was simply carried onto the field.

Whether negotiating wages or win bonuses, the fundamentals are identical:

- Do your homework.
- Lead with clarity.
- End with integrity.

Because once the ink dries, you'll face your reflection —
not your rival.

LRD360° Insight: A deal signed in ego will cost you in ethics.

Leadership, Loyalty, and Legacy on the Field

In the NFL, the difference between a headline and a
footnote can come down to a single clause.

A loyalty bonus here, a buyout there. The numbers
change, but the principle never does: What people value
most is not money, it's meaning. That's what makes these
negotiations so alive.

Each party guards a vision of legacy. The franchise
protects its culture. The agent protects the player's value.
Somewhere between the two lies the fragile concept of
loyalty, a word tossed around like confetti but rarely
honored when the scoreboard reads 0–4.

*LRD360° Insight: Loyalty isn't written in ink; it's proven in
timing.*

The Human Stakes

It's easy to forget that beneath every multimillion-dollar
contract is a human life.

An assistant coach uprooting his family for another
"one-year deal." A veteran player wondering if the next
injury will be his last. A rookie who's been told since Pop

Warner that football is his ticket to freedom.

Money can't quiet the anxiety of a profession built on expiration dates. That's why every negotiation, even the smallest, carries emotional weight.

When negotiating on behalf of an undrafted free agent, his signing bonus was barely enough to cover moving expenses. But for him, it meant validation. It meant someone believed. The fight for that bonus was waged like it was seven figures, because to him, it was priceless.

LRD360° Insight: The dollar amount may vary; the dignity never should.

Ego, Power, and Respect

When the stakes turn personal, ego rarely stays silent.

Ego is the unspoken participant in every deal; it sits quietly at the head of the table. Agents want respect. Teams want control. Players want acknowledgment. When any side feels disrespected, logic leaves the room.

That's why preparation and composure matter as much as analytics. You can't out-argue an insult; you can only out-lead it. I've seen seasoned negotiators lose millions because they let emotion drive the counter. They wanted to win the call, not the career. But real professionals understand the long game: the best deal is one you can revisit without resentment and that doesn't harm the player.

LRD360° Insight: Never let pride write a clause your client can't live with.

Culture Over Contract

In professional sports, the deal on paper only works if it aligns with the deal in practice.

Culture is the hidden variable; and narrative is how that culture is sold. Teams talk about "family," "grit," or "next man up," but behind every slogan is a story about what they truly value.

A great negotiator reads both: the written contract and the unwritten one.

You can't protect a player in a culture that treats loyalty like leverage.

And you can't build trust in a story that doesn't match behavior.

That's where leadership shows: in making sure the numbers and the narrative tell the same truth.

LRD360° Insight: Culture writes the contract. Narrative decides if anyone believes it.

Crossing Lines Without Losing Integrity

There are moments in every negotiation when both sides are technically right and ethically tested.

A general manager once told an agent, "We'll add the bonus language verbally, not in writing. You have my word." Then came the pause, the kind that separates amateurs from professionals. The player trusted him. But the agent's job was to protect trust, not depend on it.

"Then there's no harm in putting your word on paper," the agent replied. The general manager laughed, then agreed. Both knew what was at stake. Integrity isn't adversarial; it's foundational. The same principle that underpins labor agreements applies here: What's fair must also be formalized.

LRD360° Insight: If a promise can't live on paper, it won't survive reality.

Loyalty in a League That Trades It

Every season, headlines remind us how fragile loyalty can be.

A coach fired after a playoff run. A player released days after restructuring his contract "for the team." A veteran mentor replaced by a cheaper rookie. But loyalty still exists, just in smaller, quieter moments.

The team that honors a contract even after an injury. The coach who ensures a player's family is supported during transitions. The agent who tells a client the hard

truth rather than the easy sell. That's where the LRD360° Strategy lives: in those moments when doing right conflicts with doing easy.

LRD360° Insight: Loyalty is not a clause; it's a character trait.

The Currency of Trust

Trust, like salary cap space, is finite. Once it's overspent, rebuilding takes time.

Negotiations that honor trust yield better long-term outcomes. Players perform better. Coaches stay longer. Teams attract talent. Why? Because transparency sustains relationships.

The greatest compliment in any deal isn't about closing; it's about conduct. One executive once said, "Even when we don't agree, I never question your word." That's the currency that compounds.

LRD360° Insight: Trust is the only currency that appreciates with use.

The Invisible Scoreboard

Negotiation in professional sports isn't just about

numbers; it's about narrative.

Teams construct stories of discipline, culture, and continuity, their visions of sustained success. Players craft their own narratives of resilience, value, and promise. The

contract becomes the shared script both sides will live by, a framework that must be coherent from beginning to end.

Behind every deal is an invisible scoreboard: a measure of trust, perception, and timing. It's not found in the fine print but in how each side manages respect and reality. The most successful negotiations don't just balance dollars; they balance dignity. Because in the end, legacy isn't what you earn, it's what you represent when the game clock runs out.

LRD360° Insight: Every clause tells a story so make sure yours ends with respect.

The Universal Playbook: Applying LRD360° Across Fields

Every field has its own language of power: in sports, it's contracts and cap space; in health care, it's staffing ratios; in government, it's policy and public trust.

But strip away the jargon and you'll find the same anatomy of negotiation: people trying to be seen, heard, and valued.

That's why the principles of the LRD360° Strategy (Loyalty, Respect, and Dignity) apply everywhere. They function as a moral and operational compass whether you're bargaining in a boardroom, testifying before a budget committee, or leading a locker room of future champions.

LRD360° Insight: The setting changes; the stakes shift. But people are constant and people are the point.

Loyalty: The Invisible Anchor

In football, loyalty is tested every Sunday.

You win together, lose together, and still have to show up Monday to do it again. In leadership, it's no different. True loyalty isn't blind allegiance; it's consistency in purpose. It's saying the same thing in private that you promise in public.

Executives lose teams not because they lack intelligence, but because they lack predictability. People can't trust what they'll say next. The LRD360° leader knows that loyalty isn't about never changing course: it's about explaining why you change it. When people understand the reason behind the pivot, they stay on board, even in rough seas.

LRD360° Insight: Loyalty doesn't mean standing still; it means standing by your values.

Respect: The Nonnegotiable Currency

Respect is often mistaken for agreement. It's not. It's recognition that the other person's role, effort, and perspective have value even when you disagree.

In sports, the best agents respect the team's constraints. In labor relations, the best unions respect the organization's mission.

In leadership, respect is measured by how power is handled, not when it's gained, but when it could be misused. When you interrupt less and listen more, you change the tone of the room. When you acknowledge someone's preparation, you lower defenses and elevate dialogue. Respect earns cooperation where authority only demands compliance.

LRD360° Insight: Authority can be assigned; respect must be earned daily.

Dignity: The Silent Force

Dignity is the least discussed and most powerful force in negotiation. It's the energy that keeps people engaged when the money or morale runs low.

In one deal, a player's mother sat in the background quietly taking notes. When the team tried to downplay a guarantee clause, she whispered to him, "Don't let them tell you what you're worth." He nodded, lifted his head, and held his ground. That was dignity in motion — not defiance, but presence.

The same applies everywhere. When people feel dignity in their work, they protect it. They produce more, think better, and lead more strongly. A pay raise is transactional; dignity is transformational.

LRD360° Insight: Dignity is the contract no one signs but everyone remembers.

From Locker Room to Life

Every negotiation, every deal, every huddle carries one universal truth: You can't win alone.

That's as true for the quarterback as it is for the chief HR officer or union steward. The job of a leader, and a negotiator, is to make sure everyone on the team feels essential, even when they aren't the star.

That's what makes LRD360° not just a framework, but a philosophy of movement. Whether you're calling plays or crafting policy, the mission remains the same: align hearts, manage egos, and move the organization forward.

LRD360° Insight: Championships, contracts, and change all begin with conversation.

Translating the Locker Room to the Boardroom

Sports teach discipline, data analysis, and teamwork; the same skills to which great executives rely. The difference is pacing.

In football, you get four quarters to prove yourself; in public leadership, you get four fiscal years. But the rhythm is identical: plan, execute, adjust, repeat.

A head coach reviews game film; a leader reviews metrics. Both ask: What went right, what failed, and how do we fix it? That's why the LRD360° Strategy resonates across every sector. It doesn't tell leaders to mimic coaches; it reminds them to prepare like them.

LRD360° Insight: Great leaders review the game tape, even when the cameras are off.

Negotiation as Culture, Not Event

One of the biggest misconceptions about negotiation, in sports or labor, is that it happens only at the table.

The truth is every interaction before and after formal sessions shapes the outcome.

An email sent in haste can undo three months of preparation. A tone-deaf comment can shift an entire caucus against you. That's why culture must be treated as a living contract, not just between parties, but within teams.

The way you communicate, delegate, and celebrate all send signals about how you'll bargain later.

LRD360° Insight: If you only negotiate when the cameras are on, you've already lost.

Smart leaders build "trust credit" year-round so that when the next hard conversation comes, they can spend it wisely and not go into debt with their own team.

Bridging the Public and Private Playbooks

The sports world thrives on metrics: yards gained, points scored, salaries earned. The public sector thrives on service: equity, accountability, community. But both succeed only when leadership connects data to purpose.

A rookie coach once struggled to adapt to a new organization. The advice given to him was simple:

"Stop managing like you're protecting your résumé and start leading like you're protecting people."

He did, and within one season, the team culture changed.

The same shift happens in any agency or company that replaces policy memorandums with genuine mentorship. AI may run the numbers, but people still run the mission.

LRD360° Insight: Data drives results; purpose drives people.

Closing Reflection: Beyond the Numbers

Looking back at my time negotiating with zeros on the line, the numbers have faded, but the voices remain.

The tension.

The respect earned through honesty.

The quiet dignity of the moment a client said, "Thank you for fighting for me like I mattered."

That's the essence of leadership, not authority, not applause, but advocacy.

The zeros will fade, but the integrity never will.

LRD360° Insight: The best deals aren't the richest; they're the ones that make everyone richer in trust.

Epilogue: The Legacy of Leadership

The Echo After the Table

The room always feels heavier after it's over.

The table that once held laptops, coffee cups, and tension now holds silence. Papers are stacked in neat piles, pens rolled into corners, chairs tucked in. It's as if the air itself is exhaling: exhausted, relieved, unsure.

That quiet hum that follows every long negotiation is not absence; it's the echo of choices.

Because what happened at the table wasn't just about language or leverage. It was about people; their hopes, their fears, their trust in you to do right by them when no one else could see the full picture.

That echo follows every true leader. It lives in the hallways, in the tone of morning briefings, in the way employees glance at one another when your name comes up. It's invisible but undeniable. It is the resonance of how you led when it mattered most.

LRD360° Insight: Leadership doesn't end when the meeting adjourns; it echoes in every action that follows.

The Weight of the Aftermath

There's a moment after every agreement, a fleeting one, when you realize leadership isn't the roar of the fight but the calm that follows.

It's the moment when the adrenaline fades and you're left asking yourself quietly: Did I lead with courage or convenience?

In those seconds, the real reflection begins. Because even the best-drafted contract can't compensate for a broken tone. Even a perfect strategy can't outlast a failure of trust.

You walk out of the room, and suddenly leadership becomes solitary again. The cameras are gone. The talking points have been said. What remains is conscience. And that never leaves the room.

The most seasoned leaders learn to sit in that stillness. They don't rush to fill it with noise. They study it.

Because in that pause, you can hear the truth: what worked, what didn't, and what must change before the next storm comes.

LRD360° Insight: Silence isn't the absence of progress; it's the sound of wisdom arriving.

When Leadership Becomes Legacy

Legacy isn't a speech.

It's a sequence of small decisions repeated long enough to build culture.

It's how you answer the phone when the caller is angry. It's whether you tell the truth when it's inconvenient. It's how you treat the person with no title, no leverage, and no platform. They are always watching.

The myth of leadership is that legacy happens later. In truth, it's happening now. Every choice leaves a fingerprint. Every word shapes the climate that will outlast you.

When people say "We did this together" years after you're gone, that's legacy.

When they still use your language to solve new problems, that's legacy.

When they reference your name not in memory but as a method, "She would've handled it this way," that's the immortality of influence.

LRD360° Insight: Legacy is what they build when you're no longer there to lead.

www.ingramcontent.com/pod-product-compliance
Lightning Source LLC
Chambersburg PA
CBHW070525200326
41519CB00013B/2929